CULTURES OF THE WORLD

SUDAN

Patricia Levy

MARSHALL CAVENDISH
New York • London • Sydney

Reference edition reprinted 2000 by
Marshall Cavendish Corporation
99 White Plains Road
Tarrytown
New York 10591

Originated and designed by
Times Books International, an imprint of
Times Media Private Limited, a member of the
Times Publishing Group

Printed in Singapore

Library of Congress Cataloging-in-Publication Data:
Levy, Patricia Marjorie, 1951–
    Sudan / Patricia Levy.
       p. cm.—(Cultures Of The World)
    Includes bibliographical references (p.) and index.
    Summary: Examines the geography, history, government,
    economy, and culture of the war-torn country where the
    African and Arab worlds mingle.
    ISBN 0-7614-0284-5 (lib. bdg.)
    1. Sudan—Juvenile literature. [1. Sudan.] I. Title.
    II. Series.
DT154.6.L48 1997
  962.4—dc20   96–20493
                  CIP
                  AC

INTRODUCTION

THE PLACE WHERE AFRICAN AND ARAB cultures mingle, Sudan is home to a physically, religiously, and culturally diverse people. For centuries southern Sudan was a rich source of gold, slaves, and ivory for the Arab merchants of the north. As a result of this exploitation, Sudan today is tragically torn by a civil war between the Arab-dominated northern groups and the diverse black African tribal population of the south. Once a wealthy country of great cities and sheikhdoms, Sudan's many resources have been drained by the war or left undiscovered, and it is now one of Africa's poorest nations. Until the opposing sides can live peacefully, this vast country and its friendly, hospitable people will suffer the pain and hardships of war and famine. This volume of *Cultures of the World* examines Sudan's rich cultural heritage and its current problems.

CONTENTS

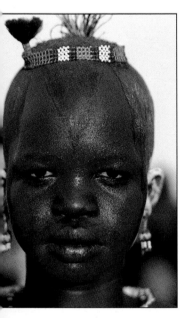

A young girl of the Dinka tribe, with her face painted for a special occasion.

CONTENTS

Arabs make up the largest ethnic group in Sudan.

GEOGRAPHY

SUDAN IS THE LARGEST COUNTRY IN AFRICA, around one third the size of the United States with a land area of nearly a million square miles. It is also the least populated, with a population of about 28 million. It is bordered by Egypt, Libya, Chad, the Central African Republic, Zaire, Uganda, Kenya, Ethiopia, and Eritrea, and part of its northeastern border lies along the Red Sea.

Sudan can be divided into four distinct geographical regions. In the north is desert, covering about 30% of the country's total land area. South of the desert is semiarid grassland and low hills covering most of central Sudan. Farther south is a vast swamp known as the Sudd, while the extreme south is rainforest. There are several low mountain ranges around the borders of the country. The River Nile, flowing from south to north, is the central feature of the country.

Opposite: **Water is scarce in the desert and savannah away from the Nile.**

Below: **The Nile at Tutti Island, near Khartoum.**

Ferries transport people and goods to villages on the banks of the Nile.

THE NILE

Giving Sudan its very existence, the Nile is the most important feature of life in the country. Its waters, which can give life to the land, can also be destructive. The Nile is the longest river in the world: its remotest headstream is in Burundi, in Central Africa, and from that point until it enters the Mediterranean Sea the river is 4,145 miles (6,670 km) long.

The Nile first enters Sudan at Nimule on the border with Uganda, where it becomes known as the White Nile. It flows sluggishly through tropical jungle to Juba, a frontier-style town, and continues north to Gondoko, where the river gains speed, passing over a series of unnavigable rapids. From there it flows into the Sudd, a vast swamp, and becomes a series of changing channels through thick beds of reeds and mud banks. North of the Sudd the river is joined by the Bahr al Ghazal and the Sobat rivers. At Khartoum, the capital of Sudan, it joins the Blue Nile.

The Blue Nile is a much more turbulent river. It has its origins in Lake Tana, a crater lake in the highlands of Ethiopia. It enters Sudan through a gorge that is almost a mile (1.5 km) deep in places. This gorge was not mapped until the 1960s because it is so inaccessible. The river crosses the flat hot plains of eastern Sudan to join the White Nile at Khartoum. The Blue Nile carries far more water than the White Nile and is the reason why the Nile never dries up. It provides most of the Middle Nile's water through the long, hot summers, and irrigates 70% of the total irrigated land in Sudan.

Two hundred miles (322 km) north of Khartoum the Nile meets the Atbara River, a major tributary. The Atbara flows for only about half the year, during the rainy season. When it floods it carries with it much of the rich black soil that once made the Nile Delta, in Egypt, so fertile. Since the Aswan Dam was built near the border of Egypt and Sudan, this rich silt no longer reaches the delta but builds up around the shores of the dam.

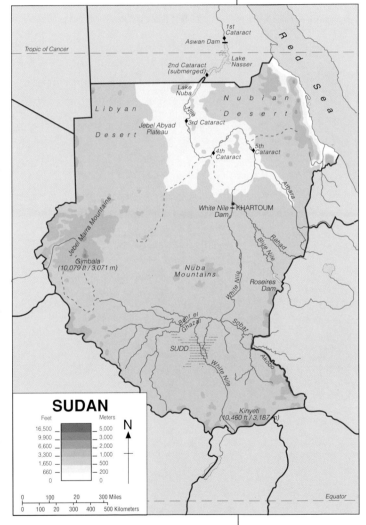

9

THE MIDDLE NILE

The Middle Nile is a distinct geographical region that extends from the meeting of the Blue Nile and the White Nile at Khartoum to the First Cataract at Aswan in Egypt. It is in turn divided geographically by several cataracts (series of rapids).

The lifeblood of the region is the river itself; it is used for irrigation—water is pumped into irrigation systems—and deposits fertile soil in the Nile floodplain, which is cultivated in the drier seasons. Irrigation along

Desert lies just beyond this strip of fertile irrigated land.

CONTROLLING THE RIVER

Egypt first built a dam at Aswan in 1902; its height was raised in 1963, which affected the lives of 50,000 Sudanese. As the waters rose 27 villages and the town of Wadi Halfa were submerged. The people were compensated and relocated at Khasm el Girba, east of Khartoum. Lake Nasser, created by the dam, is one of the world's largest reservoirs. Under an international agreement Sudan is allowed to draw 20.5 billion cubic feet of water from Lake Nasser, making major development projects possible.

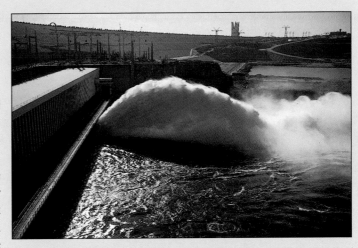

South of Khartoum are the Sennar Dam, built after World War I, and a dam at Jabal Awliya, built in 1937. The Roseires irrigation project, located on the Blue Nile and served by the Roseires Dam, has brought 864,850 acres (350,260 hectares) of land under cultivation. Another major project, abandoned in the 1990s because of the civil war, was the Jonglei canal. This canal was intended to divert some of the water of the White Nile where it makes a large bend north of Juba. Environmentalists believed that the canal would have caused a large area of the Sudd to dry up, killing the wildlife in the area.

the banks of the river creates a narrow strip of vegetation quite different from that of the surrounding area. In some places the strip is only 110 yards (100 meters) wide; in others it is nonexistent—the desert comes right to the edge of the river. As a result of desert sandstorms there is a build up of sand on the west bank of the river. This shifting sand continually encroaches on irrigated fields and settlements.

On either side of this fertile, cultivated strip is a vast area of savannah (semiarid grassland) where the inhabitants are nomadic herders who travel around the area to find fodder for their animals. As drought and the encroaching desert reduce the area of grassland, the herders have experienced serious hardship, loss of animals, and starvation.

DESERT

About 30% of Sudan's total land area is desert. To the west is the Libyan Desert, which has supplied vast amounts of oil farther west in Libya. The Nubian Desert is a region in northeast Sudan, known locally as Batn el Hagar or "the belly of stones."

Sudan is undergoing a period of rapid desertification because of the harsh demands being made on the savannah. Plants are unable to survive drought, the harvesting of firewood, and grazing by animals.

MOUNTAINS

There are four major mountainous areas in Sudan.

The Red Sea Hills, in the northeast, are low-lying wooded hills near the coast. The terrain here is quite unlike the rest of Sudan.

The Jebel Marra, mountains in the west, are distinctive, rounded pillars of rock that stand out over the lower wooded slopes. The highest point of the range is an extinct volcano called Gimbala at 10,079 feet (3,071 meters). It has hot springs, waterfalls, and mountain pools. Inside the crater itself is a lake colored green by sulphur.

In the center of the country are the Nuba Mountains, and to the south are the Immatong and Dingotona ranges. Sudan's highest peak is Mount Kinyeti at 10,460 feet (3,187 meters), close to the border with Uganda.

Within the desert are oases, small areas of land that support a tiny amount of life. El Obeid is a large oasis town whose water supply often dries up completely, making it dependent on trucked-in water.

Below: **The Red Sea Hills.**

CLIMATE

Sudan is Africa's hottest country. The northern third of the country, the Nubian and Libyan deserts, are dry all year. They experience occasional flash thunderstorms that last just a few minutes and which, in some areas, may occur only once in a generation. Temperatures range from 100°F to 113°F (38–45°C) between May and September, but can fall to almost 32°F (0°C) between November and March. Wind blows continually from the north, often whipping up sandstorms known

A school teacher walks on desert sand dunes that have engulfed an entire village.

as *haboobs* ("ha-BOOBS"), which last for a short time, darkening the sky and bringing gale-force winds. They are rarely accompanied by rain.

The middle third of the country and the south experience a wet and a dry season. The southwest experiences the highest rainfall. The rainy season starts in April and lasts until November; it provides as much as 57 inches (145 cm) of rain per year. As one travels north the rainy season grows shorter. Khartoum, at the very edge of the desert, has the least rain— on average about 8 inches (20 cm) between July and August. Temperatures are highest just before the rainy season and lowest during December and January. In Khartoum the average temperature is 89°F (32°C) in July and 74°F (23°C) in December.

The Red Sea area has a climate determined by its position on the coast. It has two rainy seasons, one in the winter and the other corresponding to the summer rainy season of the Middle Nile.

The Sudd, with its abundant water and vegetation, is home to many species of animals.

THE SUDD

The Sudd is a swamp covering about 9,000 square miles (23,310 square km), roughly the size of Wales in the United Kingdom, and slightly larger than the state of New Hampshire in the Unites States.

For thousands of years it stood as a physical barrier between the north and south of Sudan, halting the earliest recorded search for the source of the Nile, sent by the Roman emperor Nero in A.D. 60, and every other search until the 19th century. In the early 20th century the British cut a permanent waterway through the Sudd. It is still navigable today. The few travelers who make the journey see mile after mile of swamp, dominated by papyrus palm.

The Jonglei canal project, now abandoned, would have destroyed the Sudd, because the water that feeds it would have been channeled into irrigation projects to the northwest. The Sudd is one of the few remaining areas of its kind in the world, and its destruction would have decimated many species that depend on it. Halting the canal project has given the Sudd a reprieve, but at the same time farming projects that might have provided food and prevented starvation were lost.

PAPYRUS

The papyrus palm flourishes in the Sudd, dominating the landscape and gradually helping to create a surface solid enough for animals to walk across. It is a member of the sedge family and needs very moist, swamp-like conditions to survive. It grows to about 10 feet (3 meters) in height and has long woody roots that have a strong perfume and which spread under the surface of the water, anchoring the tall plant.

The papyrus formed an important part of the ancient civilizations of Sudan and Egypt. Its roots were dried and used for fuel, while the pith in the stem was, and still is, boiled and eaten. The pith was also the raw material from which paper was made. It was sliced into strips and laid out lengthwise, and other layers were put over it crosswise. The whole fabric was moistened, pressed, dried, and rubbed smooth. It was made into rolls of paper 20 feet (6 meters) in length.

Besides paper, papyrus was also used to make boxes, shoes, and even boats. A man called Thor Heyerdahl built such a boat in 1970 and sailed it from North Africa to the West Indies.

Above: **Elephants still live in the wildlife parks of southern Sudan.**

Opposite: **The thick trunk of the baobab tree is sometimes hollowed out and used as a water tank.**

FAUNA

Sudan has an enormous variety of wildlife, the result of its varied habitats —from desert to the swampy Sudd to the rainforests of the south.

In the south animals such as zebras, lions, leopards, gazelles, antelopes, and many kinds of primates still survive in the wild. Crocodiles and hippopotamuses can be seen in the Nile.

There are herds of wild elephants in what remains of wildlife parks such as Nimule in southern Sudan. The shortage of ivory caused by world bans has brought about a lucrative industry in Sudan. Poachers take advantage of the war to kill elephants for their ivory, and there is a direct trade of ivory for weapons between the southern fighters and whomever they can get weapons from. It is thought that about 10,000 elephants a year die by this means.

The wildlife in the Nuba Mountains has also suffered. As part of a scorched earth policy in the war against the Nuba, most of the animals that might have been hunted for food have been destroyed.

FLORA

The flora of the region varies as widely as does its animal life. In the south is rainforest, areas where huge buttressed trees block out the sunlight and smaller shade-loving plants survive beneath. North of the papyrus swamps of the Sudd, the plant life becomes more and more dependent on the river for its survival, forming a thin strip of vegetation along the river banks.

In the Middle Nile are large areas of savannah, sandy soil covered by tall grasses and low drought-resistant trees. The seasonal rains bring a sudden burst of life to the plants here. Of all the land in Sudan, the savannah is under the most intense pressure from drought, the cutting of firewood, and over-grazing.

Farther north little plant life grows except during occasional rain showers that allow dormant seeds to quickly germinate, flower, and produce seed, which then lie dormant, waiting for the next rain.

An interesting plant that grows in the south and the Middle Nile is the baobab tree. Its huge trunk may grow to a diameter of 30 feet (9 meters). It produces an edible fruit that is made into a cooling drink. The bark is very fibrous and is harvested for rope-making.

Another plant with a multiplicity of uses is the date palm, which can be seen all along the banks of the Nile and in the oases. Besides its edible fruit, its leaves, fibers, trunk, and sap are used to make baskets, mats, crates, furniture, sawdust, brooms, rope, roofbeams, footbridges, and wine.

Tamarisk trees exude an edible honey-like substance called manna, *thought to be the manna eaten by the Israelites in their flight from Egypt.*

MAJOR TOWNS

Khartoum, the capital of Sudan, has a mixture of Arabic, colonial, and modern buildings.

The capital city of Sudan is Khartoum; with its neighboring city of Omdurman and suburbs, it has a population of about 1.5 million. These cities, on either side of the Nile, form the industrial, commercial, and communications center of Sudan.

The British laid out Khartoum's gardens and tree-lined avenues, and many of the old colonial buildings built by the British are still in use, although they are rather shabby now. Beside these, more modern multistory buildings have sprung up. Omdurman and parts of Khartoum are more Arab in style, with flat-roofed single-story houses, narrow alleyways, beautiful mosques, and of course the *souk* ("SOOK"), the city market. Simple sailing boats carry passengers and their goods between the two cities. In the years of drought and war many refugees from southern Sudan and neighboring countries have come to the city to live in poorly-built shantytowns around the city's edge.

The second largest city in Sudan is Port Sudan (pop. 207,000) on the east coast. It was built to accommodate the trade across the Red Sea and to other coastal countries. Recently, Sudan's foreign trade has declined and the hoped for oil exports have not materialized, so Port Sudan is yet to develop fully.

Wadi Halfa, near the Egyptian border, thrives on the trade between Egypt and Sudan. A considerable black market is carried on for scarce goods in this region. Buildings are traditional one-story flat-roofed buildings,

often enclosing a central courtyard with trees to create some shade in the searing heat of the afternoons.

The major town of the south is Juba, a trading post on the last navigable point on the Nile before the border with Uganda. The British traders and missionaries who constructed the town built cathedrals, large bungalows with gardens, and wide boulevards shaded by trees. The buildings are still there, although affected by lack of use and the climate. Like Port Sudan and Khartoum, Juba has large shantytowns set up by nomadic herders displaced by the war. Various aid groups are stationed in Juba from time to time, but many have left because of the fighting. Few flights travel to Juba's small airport since one or two have been shot down.

Port Sudan is the country's major trading port on the Red Sea.

HISTORY

SUDAN IS A COUNTRY WITH TWO very distinct ethnic and geographical areas. Its history from the earliest times reflects that division. The north and middle areas of Sudan, north of Khartoum, have a fairly well-recorded history linked with the Egyptian empires. The known history of the south covers a much shorter period of only a few hundred years.

THE MIDDLE NILE

The area of modern Sudan known as the Middle Nile, from Khartoum in the south to Aswan in the north, has had a special part to play in the history of the world. The earliest cities in Africa, built by the Kush civilization, developed along this stretch of the Nile. North of the Middle Nile is the Middle East and Arab culture; south lies the barrier of the Sudd, and beyond that is black Africa. Historically, the Nile was the only route into Africa where ivory, gold, and slaves could be bought or taken. The area remained a major trade route until the development of camel routes across the Sahara in the first millennium A.D., followed in the 16th century by sailing ships trading along the coasts of Africa.

Opposite: **The tomb of the Mahdi, who fought against British rule in Sudan.**

TRAVELERS FROM KUSH

One of the outstanding features of the people of Kush, who built the earliest cities in black Africa, was their love of travel and new ideas.

They traded with the Egyptians in the north and journeyed up the Nile as far as modern Uganda. Hints of their presence have been found as far west as Lake Chad. Through their ports on the Red Sea they traded with Arabia, East Africa, India, and perhaps even China. Wherever they went they brought back new things and new ideas. A Greek bronze head made in Alexandria has been found in the ruins of one city, and Roman influence can be seen in the pillars of a temple.

Evidence has also been found of Kushite ambassadors in Rome, and an official of the Queen of Kush is believed to have met the apostle Philip on the road from Jerusalem to Gaza.

ANCIENT HISTORY

Egyptian influence can been seen in this stone statue in the National Museum in Khartoum.

The earliest structures discovered in Sudan are in the region of the Second Cataract, near the modern Egyptian border. They are a series of forts built in the second millennium B.C. by the Egyptians.

A small city called Kerma, the oldest city of the Kush civilization, was situated at the Third Cataract between about 2000 and 1500 B.C. in a period when Egyptian influence was low. Kerma was established in one of the rare areas where river water could be channeled easily to low-lying land. It is the earliest known black African city. It had a complex social structure and rulers who were buried with large numbers of human sacrifices—the most ever found in burials anywhere in the world. The settlement included a huge cemetery, two towers used for storage and the defense of the Nile traffic, a fortified city, and a factory. It is thought that the town was a packing and assembly point for exports from the Middle Nile into Egypt.

Later, around 1500 B.C., the Egyptian empire's influence in the Middle Nile extended as far as the Fourth Cataract. Fortified towns were gradually replaced by less warlike settlements with temples dedicated to the Egyptian gods. This second wave of Egyptian influence in Kush ended around 1000 B.C., either because of political problems in Egypt itself, or possibly because of low water levels in the Nile, which would have made trade difficult.

NAPATA AND MEROË

The Kush civilization also produced the Napata kingdom around the ninth century B.C., which has left behind the ruins of temples, cemeteries, and towns. At one time this kingdom was so powerful it controlled the whole of Egypt. Napata's rulers were called pharaohs and copied Egyptian customs; decorations in temple ruins show Egyptian gods with curly hair and black African features. The society had a written language that was used on tomb inscriptions.

The kingdom of Meroë came into existence around 400 B.C., as Napata declined, and lasted for about 800 years. The ruins of Meroë reveal a palace with baths and plumbing, factories, houses, and evidence of an iron-smelting works. It was a civilization based on farming the banks of the Nile, which were lined with farms and small towns. Small pyramid-shaped tombs held the bodies of kings and queens, and a Lion Temple has exterior paintings showing the rulers of Meroë with the Lion God.

Meroë existed concurrently with the Roman domination of Egypt. It was attacked by the Roman empire in 23 B.C., suffered repeated attacks by nomadic groups in the following centuries, and was finally conquered by the Axumite empire of Ethiopia in A.D. 350.

It was during the Meroë era that the ox-drawn water-wheel came into use, enabling large, previously uninhabited areas of the Middle Nile to be irrigated and settled.

23

SELUKA, SHADOOF, AND SAQUIA

The human settlement of the Middle Nile region depended on the river. In one season the Nile could destroy crops and houses by flooding; the next it could be so low that the fields could not be irrigated and crops died. In one year it might bring rich soil down from the south to grow the next season's crops while in another year it might wash all the arable soil away. There was also the problem of getting water to the arable land. Three types of land existed, each defined by the type of irrigation system it required.

Seluka land was situated on the floodplain of the river. Each year soil and water were brought down by the river and all the farmer had to do was plant his crops, weed them, and watch them grow. The drawback of this land was that it could only be cultivated during one season.

Shadoof land was the next to develop. It was the land that lay 10 feet (3 meters) or less above the river so that water could be lifted up to it using a man-powered pivot.

Saquia land was around 25 feet (8 meters) above the level of the river and only came into cultivation after the invention of the ox-drawn waterwheel.

A fourth type of land, rare in the Sudan, was **basin land**, which lay adjacent to the river but at a lower level. River water could be channeled into it by means of a canal, or when the river overflowed.

CHRISTIANITY

By the fourth century A.D., what is now northern Sudan was settled by three major kingdoms, all of whom practiced Christianity. Christianity had spread through the Roman empire into Egypt and, much later, to Sudan.

The Nubian Christian kingdoms built beautiful churches and complex cities; the ruins of these cities are still being discovered. Houses in the cities had plumbing with hot and cold water, indoor toilets, and frescoes on the walls, and the residents drank from imported glassware.

ISLAM

Gradually this sophisticated urban lifestyle gave way to a series of sheikhdoms dominated by Arabs from the deserts east and west of the Nile. The Arab tribes brought their own religion—Islam. The largest of the sheikhdoms was the Funj kingdom of Sennar, which survived into the 19th century. The Funj sheikh's wealth came from gold mines close to the border with modern Ethiopia.

At the end of the 18th century the Arab sheikhdoms of Sudan were attacked by the ruler of Egypt, Muhammad Ali. He had seized power in Egypt with the use of a Turkish slave army, and when the army began to get bored and dangerous in Egypt he sent them south with his son to take slaves and gold. The troops ventured into and beyond the Sudd. They sent back the ears of those they killed, and 30,000 slaves. During the return journey Muhammad's son was killed, and in retribution Muhammad sent more troops and took control of Sudan. Egyptian rule lasted 50 years.

The ruins of Christian churches are still being discovered beneath the desert sands.

A 17th century French doctor visited the Funj kingdom and described the sheikh's enormous wealth and power.

SLAVERY

After the last Christian kingdom was conquered by Egypt in A.D. 652, an annual tribute of slaves was levied on the remaining Nubian settlements by the Egyptian invaders. The Arab sheikhs formalized slave-taking by arranging treaties with the Nubians to exchange slaves for Egyptian goods. Despite strong resistance to the Arab armies, slavery became a tradition that lasted for 600 years and dominated north-south relations. A form of slavery has been revived in modern times, with southern Sudanese being forced into local militias and domestic service in the north.

COLONIALISM AND THE MAHDI

Egypt went heavily into debt over the building of the Suez Canal in the 19th century, giving Britain the opportunity to intervene in the region. In 1877 General Charles Gordon was appointed governor of Sudan and Egypt.

While the British were establishing their authority, a local leader emerged. Muhammad Ahmad declared himself a *mahdi* or savior, elected by God to lead a holy war (*jihad*). He called for Sudan to be ruled according to the laws of Islam. The Mahdi took the towns of El Obeid and

Darfur by siege, starving out the troops and killing their European leaders. Hearing of the unrest, the British sent General Gordon to Khartoum to hold the city against the Mahdi. Gordon asked for reinforcements too late; the city was taken and Gordon killed. His head was put on a pole to taunt the relieving troops.

The Mahdists held power for 10 years while Britain and other colonial powers fought over other regions of Africa, dividing up the land to be exploited. Eventually a campaign against the Mahdists was organized. General Herbert Kitchener was sent with troops from Egypt, arriving in Omdurman on September 1, 1898. They were attacked by 60,000 Mahdists armed with swords and shields and wearing suits of armor. Eleven thousand Sudanese died, and the British regained power in Sudan.

Above: **The Mahdi.**

Left: **General Gordon's grand colonial headquarters building in Khartoum is now used as the Presidential Palace.**

The optimism of the Unity Monument has been undermined by decades of civil war.

INDEPENDENCE

The British and Egyptians remained in joint control of Sudan until World War II. In 1946 Britain and Egypt began negotiations to decide Sudan's future, but they ended in deadlock as Egypt demanded British withdrawal and Britain wanted to remain in control.

In 1948 the British began a process of giving Sudan the choice of union with Egypt or independence. They established a legislature, which the pro-Egyptians boycotted, and in December 1950 the legislature passed a motion asking Britain and Egypt for independence.

Meanwhile, the Egyptian parliament named King Farouk of Egypt the sole ruler of Sudan, but after his abdication in 1952 both countries agreed to give Sudan independence. In 1953 the first elections were held, and a three-year period of replacing British and Egyptian officials with Sudanese began.

CIVIL WAR

At this stage the enormous social and political differences between the north and the south began to make themselves felt. During the British administration the two halves of the country had been kept separate, but with the new pro-Egyptian party in power, southern elements began to see a threat to their control over their own affairs. In August 1955 a mutiny among southern regiments broke out but was quickly put down.

The optimism of the Unity Monument has been undermined by decades of civil war.

Sudan formally became a republic on January 1, 1956. Elections were held in February 1958 and the Umma Party, led by Abdallah Khalil, came to power. His government was formed from a coalition of small parties and was quite unstable. Within six months interparty quarrels and national strikes ended the government.

Power was assumed by General Ibrahim Abbud, the chief of staff of the armed forces. He outlawed strikes and political parties, and under this military government, which remained in power for six years, Sudan became politically stable and its economy began to improve.

A low-key rebellion continued in the south. Finally there was an unarmed mass rebellion against the military rulers and they agreed to step down. Elections followed and in May 1965 parliamentary rule was reestablished.

Sudan became a member of the Arab League in January 1956 and a member of the United Nations in November of the same year.

Southern villages lie deserted after raids by both government and rebel troops. Their occupants fled to refugee camps and shantytowns.

Islamic law forbids the consumption of alcohol. When Nimeiry declared shariah law, the entire Sudanese stock of alcohol was poured into the Nile.

NIMEIRY

In 1969 a second coup brought Colonel Jaafar al-Nimeiry to power. Political parties were again banned and a degree of economic stability returned. This military government withstood 24 further attempted coups. One of the most optimistic aspects of Nimeiry's rule was the peace accord he made with the southern forces at Addis Ababa in 1972, which gave the south a large amount of autonomy and halted the war.

Nimeiry began a series of projects to make Sudan a major food supplier, including the Jonglei canal project. But his loans from the International Monetary Fund caused dissent when he was forced to raise food prices to meet debt repayments.

To gain support wherever he could, Nimeiry turned to the conservative northern Islamic groups, declaring shariah ("sha-RI-ah") law in 1983. This meant that throughout the country every citizen, regardless of religion, was bound by the laws of Islam.

Angered by the imposition of Islamic laws, the non-Muslim rebels in the south took up arms once more. They were led this time by John Garang, a U.S. economics graduate, who formed the SPLA (Southern People's Liberation Army). Control of the south was quickly lost to the southerners and a state of emergency was declared.

In 1985 there was a successful coup, and Sayyid Sadiq al-Mahdi, great-grandson of the Mahdi, became the new leader of Sudan.

A billboard promoting President Nimeiry.

BASHIR

For the next four years there was a return to civilian parliamentary government and a purge of Islamic extremists. But shariah law continued, and food shortages and economic decline were made worse by drought and the war in the south. Another military coup took place in 1989, led by Brigadier Omar Hassan al-Bashir. He declared a state of emergency, political opposition was suppressed, and the war against the south was stepped up. Moves toward democracy began again in 1993, but most people consider these changes to be purely cosmetic.

Sudan in the 1990s has been faced with drought, starvation, the influx of refugees from its warring neighbors, civil war, a collapsed economy, military rule, shariah law, and human rights abuses. In November 1995 all humanitarian flights into the south were banned, probably as part of a final solution to the problem of the south.

President Bashir reviews the troops at his government's inauguration.

GOVERNMENT

SUDAN HAS EXPERIENCED MANY FORMS of government over the centuries, from small city states ruled by a king or queen to rule by foreign powers, from parliamentary democracy to military juntas. In modern times it is a politically and socially diverse country with many small factional groups vying for control. Successive governments have had to form coalitions with powerful interest groups in order to maintain power. The most powerful groups of all are the northern Islamic organizations. Their influence resulted in the adoption of shariah law in 1983. The brief spell of peace between the north and south ended when the southern groups saw this as a dismissal of the peace they had made in 1972. Sudan has subsequently experienced full-scale civil war between government troops and the Southern People's Liberation Army.

Opposite: **A soldier of the Southern People's Liberation Army (SPLA).**

Left: **Marchers carry pictures of John Garang and former president Nimeiry in a political rally.**

Sudan alienated many of its overseas political allies by declaring its support for Iraq in the Gulf War.

THE STRUCTURE OF GOVERNMENT

Theoretically Sudan is a parliamentary democracy. In the last decade it has been a one-party presidential republic, a military regime, a parliamentary democracy, another military regime, and a transitional state between military rule and parliamentary democracy. Currently a parliament exists, but it has no representatives from the south and most of its members were appointed by the current military ruler, General Omar Hassan al-Bashir. Elections are due but have not yet taken place.

THE PRESIDENCY

When parliamentary democracy is in effect, the government of Sudan has a strong presidency. The president theoretically holds office for six years, although coup attempts often interrupt this process.

After the 1985 coup, when Sudan spent a brief time as a democracy, there was no president. Instead the role was carried out by a five-man Supreme Council.

As of 1996 the presidency is held by General Bashir. He is also prime minister, commander of the Armed Forces, and was leader of the Supreme Military Council that elected him president. He has the power to suspend the constitution and declare a state of emergency, a prerogative which has been used several times by Sudanese presidents.

Politicians at a pre-election conference in Port Sudan.

34

THE LEGISLATURE

In its democratic state the legislature was a single body of 24 representatives, partly elected and partly appointed by the president. Elections were held by secret ballot. There was universal suffrage. The government was formed by the party with the majority of seats in the parliament, from which an executive cabinet of ministers and a prime minister were elected.

Currently the legislative authority is called the Transitional National Assembly, although elections have not yet taken place and many of its members were also members of the Supreme Military Council. A new cabinet made up of appointed civilians has also been formed.

The National Assembly in Khartoum.

THE CONSTITUTION

The constitution is currently suspended. When it is in operation it allows for freedom to form political parties and freedom of speech. It describes the presidency, the legislature, and the judiciary. For a time after 1973 there was a separate Southern Regional Constitution, which established a Southern Legislative Body whose chairman was vice-president of Sudan. Its scope encompassed all regional matters but excluded national and foreign affairs. This Southern Legislative Body is also currently suspended.

An amendment to the constitution needed a two-thirds vote in the National Assembly. An amendment to the Southern Regional Constitution needed a four-fifths vote of the National Assembly as well as presidential approval.

Few of the Islamic laws have been imposed in the south, primarily because the government cannot enforce them, but non-Muslims living in the north have been punished under these laws.

THE JUDICIARY

Since the adoption of shariah law the judiciary has become quite a complex institution. It has two major branches, civil and shariah.

The civil branch of the judiciary has a Higher Judicial Council headed by the president, who appoints the judges. Under the 1973 Judiciary Act, which is still in place, civil law cases are decided by the Supreme Court, the Courts of Appeal, and provincial courts. The Supreme Court also interprets the constitution when it is in operation. Criminal cases are heard by the major courts, minor courts, and magistrate courts. The major courts can impose the death sentence.

Paralleling the civil courts are the shariah courts, which decide on civil matters affected by Islamic law.

SHARIAH LAW

Penalties determined by shariah law apply to all citizens, regardless of their own religion. Public lashing is common for those found guilty of drinking alcohol or uttering blasphemy, for which the maximum sentence is 100 lashes. For a theft of anything valued over US$40, the right hand is amputated. For aggravated theft or more serious crimes, the right hand and left foot are amputated. Public hanging takes place for crimes such as armed robbery.

Adultery and repeated homosexuality are also punishable by execution, but in both cases the enormous burden of proof has prevented these punishments being carried out. Those convicted of shameful acts are lashed; this is quite common in cases of suspected adultery.

Those injured by crime can demand retribution. For example, a woman whose arm was broken demanded that the arm of the woman who caused the injury be broken also.

LAW ENFORCEMENT

Sudan has a national police force under the command of the president and administered by the Ministry of the Interior. The police force is about 11,000 people strong and is divided for administrative purposes into regions, each with its own Commandant of Police. There are foot and mounted brigades, some patrolling their beat on camels and mules. There are about 1.5 police per thousand of the population.

There is a second force policing Sudan under the Ministry of State Security, which is responsible for collecting information on state security.

The police force is responsible for internal security, criminal investigation, and the administration of migration, nationality, and the registration of foreigners. Outside of crimes caused as a direct result of the war, the most common crimes are animal theft and tribal disputes.

A Shilluk king and his bodyguards. In isolated areas, especially in the south, federal laws give way to tribal customs and local militia.

LOCAL GOVERNMENT

Like all the other institutions described in this chapter, the organization of local government is subject to change. Under its constitution Sudan is divided into 18 provinces, 12 in the north and six in the south. Each provincial government is headed by a governor and has a council that is partly elected and partly nominated by national government and local interest groups. Each local government has a small budget.

POLITICAL PARTIES

Political parties in Sudan undergo periods of being banned interspersed with periods of relative freedom. At the moment Sudan is in an intermediate state with elections promised, in which case all political parties will be legitimate again.

In times of political freedom there are up to 30 different parties, and all democratic governments have been made up of coalitions of these parties. The most prominent is the Umma Party, followed by the Democratic Unionist Party, both of which are centrist/right-wing Muslim groups. Other significant groups are the Muslim Brotherhood, which holds fundamentalist views about law, order, and the place of religion; the Sudan National Party, which represents Christian and non-Muslim people; and the Communist Party.

No parties represent the south in the democratic process because the southern rebels have refused to take part. The political groups of the south are collectively known as Anya Nya II. The main group is divided into military and civilian wings, the SPLA (Southern People's Liberation Army) and the SPLF (Southern People's Liberation Front). Both groups are led by John Garang (pictured right).

An SPLA officer and his troops.

HUMAN RIGHTS

Sudan has a record of human rights abuses by both government and southern forces. Government security forces are said to operate "ghost houses," secret detention centers where political opponents are taken for interrogation. Amnesty International has recorded many cases of illegal detention and torture of political opponents of the government.

Amnesty International also blames both government and rebel forces for the "disappearance" of thousands of civilians in the south and the Nuba Mountains. Government forces have murdered, raped, and driven millions of people from their homes. Rebel forces have also committed atrocities, especially in interfactional fighting. In 1995 thousands of people fled from Sudan into northern Uganda, and there were reported cases of militia crossing the border to take men they considered deserters. Boys as young as 12 years old have been kidnapped and pressed into the southern militias or into a form of slavery in the north of Sudan.

An SPLA officer and his troops.

ECONOMY

THE ECONOMY OF SUDAN could not be any worse. Since the mid-1960s economic growth has been nil. Inflation is running at 45–75%; some estimates suggest the figure is much higher. Huge international debts, war, famine, the withdrawal of foreign firms, drought, and the influx of foreign refugees have brought about a near-impossible situation. Sudan is one of the poorest and least developed countries in the world.

During the years of relative stability in the 1970s it seemed for a while that Sudan's vast potential could be tapped. The south has unexploited and untold reserves of oil and minerals, vast areas of land that could be irrigated to produce crops, and energy to be tapped from the force of the Nile's waters.

Many foreign countries were willing to invest in exploration and development projects, but the war with the south and instability in the north have brought most of the major development projects to a standstill. The Jonglei canal, once near completion, is abandoned, the expensive digging machinery destroyed and the trench refilled with sand. If completed it would have provided an enormous area where cash crops for export or, better still, crops to feed the hungry of Sudan could have been grown. Similarly the oil companies that were searching for oil have left because control of the south is in the hands of the SPLA and planes can no longer fly safely. Riverboat services through the Sudd to Juba have also ended for security reasons.

Above: **An artisan at work in Omdurman.**

Opposite: **Even children, like this girl with her bundle of rope, help in the family business.**

41

AGRICULTURE

Sudan has the potential to become a major producer of cash crops but suffers like other cash crop producers from the ups and downs of world prices. Sudan has a total land area of over 618 million acres (250 million hectares) and about 12% of that is potentially prime agricultural land, but only about 13.4 million acres (5.4 million hectares) is actually cultivated. Seventy-eight percent of the labor force is engaged in agriculture, making Sudan the sixth most agriculturally-oriented country in the world. Agriculture accounts for 86% of export earnings.

The area around Khartoum is a major cotton growing area. Cotton is an important crop for Sudan, accounting for 50–60% of exports. It grows well in the hot dry climate around Khartoum, but needs constant irrigation. It is harvested largely by hand then separated from the seed cases in the local cotton ginning plants. Government development plans aim to increase the production of short-stapled cotton, a variety that can be harvested mechanically. The cotton industry was nationalized in 1970, and cotton is sold and exported through a Cotton Marketing Board.

Sorghum is another very successful

Sacks of recently harvested cotton in the El Gezira district.

Sudan is the world's second largest exporter of peanuts after the United States.

A harvest of *ful* beans is tossed in the air so that leaves and chaff are blown away by the wind.

crop in Sudan. It is a drought-resistant grain and has been the staple food of most of Africa for centuries. Besides being an important food crop for the country, it is also an export crop. The sorghum plant grows about 13 feet (4 meters) tall and bears a large flower head on which round seeds form. The seeds are ground into flour and made into porridge and flat bread; both are staple foods in Sudan. Sorghum can also be brewed into beer. Other important grains for the local market include millet and rice.

Oilseeds are a growing export industry, with about two million acres of land under production. Other crops include sugarcane, peanuts, onions, and sunflower seeds. Attempts to grow tropical crops such as tobacco, coffee, and tea in the south have been hindered by the war.

GUM ARABIC

Another lucrative crop is gum arabic, which is used as a thickening agent in cooking and when making candy, adhesives, and drugs. It is also a major ingredient in gelatin capsules. Sudan produces four-fifths of the world supply of gum arabic. It is secreted by a species of acacia tree that grows wild in western Sudan. The walnut-sized balls of rubbery matter are harvested in the dry season. Gum arabic is marketed through a company that is 30% state-owned.

THE RAHAD AND EL GEZIRA DEVELOPMENT PROJECTS

The El Gezira project, located at the junction of the Blue Nile and the White Nile, is a government development project using industrial farming techniques. Divided into large plots and rented out to cooperative groups, the area produces 60% of the country's cotton, 50% of its wheat, 12% of its sorghum, and 30% of its lubia, an animal fodder.

A similar project is being carried out at Rahad, where land is irrigated using water reserves from the Roseires Dam. The expensive project was financed by the World Bank, the United States, and Kuwait. The land is rented out to tenant farmers, and the proportion of land given to each of several crops is determined by the government. About half the land produces cotton, while the other half is planted with peanuts and vegetables, producing food for the local market as well as export crops.

The people who farm the land are the original farmers, but since the project began they must grow crops in the proportion determined by the government. The scheme has failed for this very reason. As world prices fluctuate farmers should be able to switch crops, but their agreements force them to grow crops that are not in demand. A black economy has developed where farmers secretly grow higher proportions of sorghum, which they can sell locally. They devote the fertilizer given to them to the sorghum and leave the cotton unfertilized, which results in a poor cotton crop.

LIVESTOCK

In vast areas of eastern and western Sudan nomads roam with their herds, moving from one oasis to another, cropping the land as they go. The animals are mostly cattle, camels, and goats.

More than any other section of the economy, the tending of livestock has suffered from the years of drought, famine, and war. The drought brought the herders to the cities to find water, and thousands of the animals died in the long journeys. As animals died the people who depended on them set up shantytowns around the cities or came to depend more and more on refugee camps. In the south, where there was no drought, animals have been taken by raiding troops from both sides of the war and even killed as part of a scorched earth policy, to stop southern soldiers finding food. The wealth of a family depended entirely on its animals; now thousands of families are reduced to begging.

Sudanese camel traders herd their animals just as cattle drovers once herded cattle across the American plains. Sudan has the longest droving track in the world.

A nomad girl takes camels to be watered in Darfur.

FORESTRY AND FISHING

Sudan has 3.5 million acres (1.4 million hectares) of forest, which are entirely owned by the government. The forests are logged and produce about 48 million cubic yards (37 million cubic meters) of wood per year, most of which is used for firewood. Other forestry products include beeswax, tannin, senna, and luxury woods such as mahogany.

Fishing on the Nile is an important local industry. Nile perch are readily caught from the banks and provide daily food and most of the protein for people living along the river. Dried fish are traded with nomads for milk and animal products. A fishing industry has also been encouraged along the Red Sea coast.

Below: **At Habila refugee camp an attempt is being made to grow seedlings for reforestation.**

Below right: **Net-fishing on the Blue Nile.**

Sudan Railways employs around one fifth of all wage earners in Sudan.

TRANSPORTATION

Sudan has only 1,000 miles (1,600 km) of paved roads. Most people travel on the back of open trucks, often 60 people crushed into a space in which 20 people would be cramped. Trucks travel across packed earth tracks that become swamps when it rains and extremely rough when it is dry. Many roads are impassable in the wet season.

Due to the war, there is very little river transport. Between the Third and Fourth Cataracts there is still a boat service covering about 175 miles (280 km) that operates the postal service and supplies the riverside towns with fresh produce from the cities farther south.

River transport between Juba and Khartoum has been suspended, and the only other route into Juba is by air. Flights too are often suspended, since several flights were shot down. There have been no aid flights to the south since they were banned in November 1995. Sudan's major airport is in Khartoum, with secondary airports in Juba and Port Sudan.

The government-owned Sudan Railways operates the country's limited rail system. The main line runs from El Obeid to Lake Nasser, and branch lines run from Sennar and Atbara to Port Sudan, and from El Obeid to Nyala. Sudan Railways handles almost all transportation of foreign trade.

Soap industry workers in Gedaref.

MINING

Sudan is thought to have considerable natural resources of gold, chromium, manganese, magnetite, salt, and mica, but because of the war very little exploration or large-scale mining is carried out. Mining contributes less than 0.02% of Sudan's Gross National Product and has had zero growth since 1971.

Gold has been mined for centuries in southern Sudan and in the Red Sea Hills. The west has vast untapped reserves of uranium. Chromite, a black ore from which chromium is extracted, exists near the Ethiopian border. Sudan is thought to have about 250 million tons of iron ore and 10 million tons of copper.

MANUFACTURING

Most industry in Sudan consists of food processing plants around Khartoum, particularly plants processing cottonseed and peanut oil, wheat flour, raw sugar, and gum arabic. There are also oil refineries and factories producing cement, cotton textiles, glass, paper, and light machinery.

During the 1970s the government nationalized most existing industry and confiscated several foreign-owned firms, but this policy was reversed in the 1980s and foreign investment is again encouraged.

The introduction of Islamic law in 1983 confused the issue again when it became illegal to lend money at interest. Manufacturing growth is virtually nil, and all industries lack investment and managerial skills. Sudan loses a large number of educated and skilled workers through emigration to the neighboring oil-rich countries of Libya, Saudi Arabia, the United Arab Emirates, and Kuwait. Industrial growth is also constrained by the underdeveloped and expensive transportation system.

ENERGY

Sudan has a very limited electrical generating capacity of about 1.1 billion kilowatts annually. Most towns have electricity for only a few hours a day. Out of town, electricity comes from small, individually-owned gasoline-driven generators.

Nationally, most of Sudan's electricity comes from hydroelectric power stations, with about 70% produced by the Roseires Dam on the Blue Nile. There are also thermal energy power plants that burn refined petroleum imported from neighboring countries, particularly Saudi Arabia. As in so many other aspects of life in Sudan, there is enormous potential for development and self-sufficiency, including opportunities for further hydroelectric and solar power generation.

SUDANESE

SUDAN IS AN INTERESTING PLACE because it is the point where two races meet. In the south the people are black African and live lives similar to tribespeople elsewhere in Africa, worshiping animist gods, living in mud-walled huts, farming and gathering food as their ancestors did. Many tribespeople prefer to wear nothing but jewelry.

As one travels north the appearance of the people changes to paler, olive skin and straight black hair. The round, mud-walled huts give way to mud brick one-story buildings with walled courtyards. Dress undergoes a total change, as nudity gradually gives way to complete covering. Muslims consider it irreligious to have exposed flesh, so men wear long white robes and turbans, while women wear full-length dresses covered by a wrap that leaves only their faces exposed.

Opposite: **Mother and son from a wealthy Khartoum family.**

Left: **Women attend a nutrition class.**

PEOPLE OF THE NORTH

Around 39% of Sudanese people consider themselves to be Arab, although a much larger proportion speak Arabic and live an Arabic lifestyle. Some of those who call themselves Arabs are descendants of Arabs who emigrated to Sudan, while others belong to Sudanese groups who fully adopted Arabic language and culture. The Arabs live chiefly in the north of Sudan, in settled communities and small nuclear families rather than in nomadic groups. They consider the home a very private place, but they are also very hospitable and freely offer strangers a rest and a meal. Arab people fill all walks of life in Sudan, from small farmers to city intellectuals.

A Nubian child tends goats on the banks of the Nile.

The other major group in northern Sudan are the Nubian tribes, who represent around 8% of the population of Sudan. They speak Nubian, an ancient language with its own alphabet and literature. Modern Nubians also speak Arabic. Many have been resettled in other areas of Sudan after the creation of the Aswan Dam flooded their land. They are gradually becoming assimilated into Arab culture. In appearance they are close to their Arab neighbors, with straight black hair and slightly darker skin.

BAGGARA TRIBES

The Baggara tribes are black-skinned nomads who claim Arab descent. By the 16th century nomadic Arabs from northern Africa and Arabia had migrated as far as Lake Chad and had intermarried with black Africans. In the 18th century their descendants moved to Sudan, where the land was suited to their nomadic or seminomadic lifestyle.

Traditionally they have a social system based on family ties, changing allegiances, and blood feuds. Power is not hereditary, but stems from wealth and strength of personality. Many Baggara groups today live in central Sudan. The major tribes include the Humr, Messiria, Hawazma, and Rizeigat.

A girl from Darfur in
western Sudan.

PEOPLE OF THE WEST

The mountains of western Sudan are home to the Nuba, a dark-skinned group of tribes, most of whom are Muslim. To the west again there are tribes like the nomadic Fur, a Muslim group after whom the Darfur provinces are named; the Baggara tribes, who are nomadic traders; and the Zaghawa tribe, who are black-skinned nomads. The Zaghawa regularly make the enormous trek across the desert to the Libyan border. The journey takes 27 days, crossing the Sahara. There they sell their great herds of camels and trade in salt, a rare commodity in Sudan. The Fallata Umboro tribe, southwest of Darfur, are unlike any of their neighboring tribes and are thought to have descended from the Fulani group, a Muslim nomadic tribe from northern Nigeria.

THE NUBA

The story of the Nuba people is a 20th century tragedy. Thought to have descended from the ancient Kush civilization that built the city of Meroë, they inhabit the Nuba Mountains in the midwest of Sudan. For centuries the 50 different tribes that make up the Nuba lived peacefully among themselves and with their Arab neighbors. They kept cattle and terraced the mountainsides to grow grain, vegetables, and fruit. Many of them practice an unconventional form of Islam that allows alcohol and pork, but there may be Christians and animists within the same family. They went for the most part naked.

During the 1970s and 1980s many tourists came to the area to see their tribal dances and wrestling. The government began a campaign to clothe the Nuba and force them to follow traditional Islamic rules. After several years of persecution the Nuba declared their support for the SPLA, and since then the policy of "civilizing" the Nuba has given way to eradication. The Nuba Mountains have been cut off from the rest of the world and government troops have carried out a scorched earth policy, killing and burning the Nuba's crops and animals. Whole tribes have been forced into camps where men and women are segregated, and there have been reports of rape and genocide.

In 1995 the unofficial leader of the Nuba, Youssif Kuwa Mukki, returned from exile to help his people fight for their survival and identity. Some see new hope for the Nuba, as southern troops help to set up schools and clinics where 10 years ago there were none.

PEOPLE OF THE EAST

The Rasheida are a nomadic tribe of people who arrived in the Sudan region in the early 19th century from Saudi Arabia. They live in goatskin tents in the area around Kassala. They are easily recognizable by the delicate veils worn by the women and the profusion of silver jewelry that they wear.

When a girl from the Rasheida tribe is ready to marry, she approaches the man she wants and flirtatiously lifts her veil so that he can see her chin. If he accepts her offer he must find 100 camels for her bride price. By tradition the Rasheida breed camels and goats, but in modern times many of them drive Toyota trucks.

The Beja are Muslims living in the Red Sea Hills. They became famous in Britain in the 19th century for their fierce fighting in the Mahdist battles. Although they are traditionally nomadic, some Beja have adopted a lifestyle of farming cotton. They

The heavily decorated black and silver veil identifies this woman as a member of the Rasheida tribe.

regard the sea as hostile and do not eat fish except in times of extreme need. The major Beja groups are the Bisharin, Hadebdowa, Amarar, Abdedh, and Beni Amer. Their thick, curly hair gives them quite a distinctive appearance, and those who work in the docks in Port Sudan are still distinguishable by their traditional hairstyles.

Refugees stand in front of a sea of tents at Wad Sherifa, the world's largest refugee camp.

REFUGEES

Eastern Sudan is now the permanent home of tens of thousands of refugees fleeing from war in Ethiopia. Wad Sherifa is the biggest refugee camp in the world, with a population of 60,000. Some Ethiopian and Eritrean refugees have found work in the cities as domestic servants.

Refugee camps in central and southern Sudan are filled with Sudanese people displaced by the war, as well as refugees from Chad, Uganda, and other African countries.

TRIBES AND THEIR CATTLE

Cattle herding is not just a job for the tribal people of the south. Cattle are their currency and provide food, drink, clothing, and fuel.

A Dinka's social status is determined by the number and fierceness of animals in his herd. Each year the tribes move their cattle back and forth between the river and the grasslands. When a Dinka boy comes of age he is given his first ox and takes a name determined by the appearance of the ox. The Dinka even make up songs about their cattle.

Before the Mundari were displaced by the war, looking after cattle dominated their lives. Their cattle are huge and have thick branched horns that the Mundari train to grow into intricate shapes.

PEOPLE OF THE SOUTH

The Dinka are the largest ethnic group in southern Sudan, with a population of around three million. They are nomadic herders whose lives revolve around their animals. Fiercely independent, they saw the introduction of shariah law as an attack on their way of life. While many of them try to live peacefully, many more have become soldiers of the SPLA who live deep in the jungles of the south, raiding other tribes for food, shelter, and clothes and threatening all road and air transport.

Neutral tribes have also been displaced by the war. The Mundari, who lived just south of the Sudd, are the second largest tribal group in the south after the Dinka. They were attacked by cattle-raiding Dinka and government troops in the mid-1980s and fled south to refugee camps around Juba. Some of them have taken to self-defense and carry automatic weapons. The chance of their ancient way of life surviving the war is very remote.

The Shilluk are an animist tribe who have farmed the fertile banks of the Nile south of Khartoum since the 16th century. They were driven from

A Shilluk war dance. Despite Western and Arabic influences, traditional practices remain strong in many tribes of the south.

their land by government troops who were attempting to wipe out places where the SPLA could find food or shelter. When Bettina Selby, a journalist, visited their temporary camps in the mid-1980s, she found thousands of Shilluk people near starvation. International relief organizations had set up feeding stations for children who were at the most risk of dying.

Other southern tribes include the Nuer and the Azande.

DRESS

There can be no more radical differences in dress than those that exist in Sudan.

In the cities of the north and south business is conducted in Western dress, usually a thin short-sleeved shirt and cotton trousers for men, and light cotton dresses for women. Ties and jackets are not worn even at the most formal occasions because of the high temperatures.

At home men from the north relax in the loose, long cotton shirt called a *jallabiya* ("CHAL-a-bee-ah"), loose pants, and a turban called an *emme* ("EM-ah"). They are also likely to wear this dress for formal occasions.

Many northern women wear Western clothes that are longer and cover more of the body than their Western peers might want to wear in such a climate. Out of the house they cover this with a *tobe* ("TOH-bay"), which is a 10-yard (9-meter) piece of thin fabric. It is wrapped around and around the body, covering its outlines and leaving only the face exposed. Its color is chosen to match the clothes underneath. For work a white *tobe* is worn, while women in the east of Sudan often wear brown *tobe*. In some areas in the far north the *tobe* are very colorful.

Women can be arrested for appearing in public dressed immodestly. This law is relaxed the farther south one travels.

Women in the north of Sudan cover their Western clothes with long wraps called *tobe*.

SCARRING

Scarring is a very ancient tradition in Sudan. Frescoes in the historical city of Meroë depict scarring patterns on the faces of figures. Common among the southern tribes, scars indicate a woman's age, marital status, and number of children. Men also have facial scarring, which is carried out as part of their initiation into manhood.

A common scarring pattern is a row of raised bumps across the forehead, made by rubbing ash into the wounds. The Shilluk king (pictured right) has this type of scarring. The Nuer have six parallel lines on their forehead, while a tribe called the Ja'aliin have lines marked on to their cheeks. The scarring is considered very beautiful.

Other forms of body decoration include lip tattooing, practiced by some women in the north, and painting hands and feet with intricate henna patterns.

Traditionally, the southern tribespeople wear little except for jewelry. Some (particularly older women) wear beaded aprons or sarongs. Facial scarring is widely practiced.

Because of government campaigns and the influence of missionaries, many southern tribespeople now wear clothes. The government policy of clothing the southern tribespeople has become part of the conflict between the north and the south. Southerners resent the attempts to impose Islamic laws and customs on their traditional lifestyles, while the people of the north believe that it is their religious duty to encourage the spread of Islam.

LIFESTYLE

IT IS VERY UNLIKELY that anyone in Sudan has been unaffected by the calamities of the past decade. A large portion of the population are nomadic at least part of the year, and it is perhaps these people who have been hardest hit by the years of drought and the rapid encroachment of the desert. Farmers living along the fertile banks of the Nile experienced a serious flood in the mid-1980s that did enormous damage to their homes and herds. They have also been raided by both SPLA and government troops. Groups like the Nuba have been worst hit with their very existence in danger. The general economic slump, the introduction of shariah law, and the many coups have affected everyone who tries to make a living in both the country and cities.

The major divisions in lifestyle are those between the north and south and the city and country.

People in the hot, dry north can make a living selling water carried from the river. Many women and children spend a large portion of their day finding enough water to keep themselves and their animals alive.

Opposite: **A chicken farmer at Khasm el Girba.**

Left: **A Dinka family pounds millet in front of their mud and straw hut.**

63

LIFE IN THE NORTH

During the long hot days, life in Sudanese cities is conducted at a slow pace. People not in their offices spend the afternoons in the courtyards of their traditional one-story mud-brick houses. The walls are very thick to keep the interior as cool as possible. Many people in Khartoum also live in modern Western-style apartment blocks. There are frequent power cuts, so refrigeration and air-conditioning are almost nonexistent. Most of the daily life of Khartoum is conducted out in the open under whatever shade is around. Wooden-framed string beds are pulled out of the house into the courtyard to serve as chairs.

In the city life revolves around the *souk* ("SOOK"), the city market. Khartoum's largest *souk* is across the river in Omdurman, where crafts-workers of all kinds make precious objects out of ivory, ebony, gold, or silver. More ordinary *souks* contain shops selling fresh food, tobacco, and a few electrical goods. Western-style department stores do not exist here; all food is sold fresh, and there are constant shortages of most things.

There are few women to be seen on the busy city streets (this one is in Omdurman).

Women are not often seen in the cities. They either work or stay at home, while the men do most of the grocery shopping. There are a few illegal drinking shops and many tea and coffee shops for people to while away the hot afternoons.

Khartoum's city center has skyscrapers, some big hotels, and stores catering to the dwindling number of tourists that venture this far south. Business hours are usually between 8 a.m. and 2 p.m. Everything closes during the afternoon and reopens again when it is cooler, at around 6 p.m.

In the wealthier parts of the city the houses have high fences with carefully guarded four-wheel drive cars parked outside. Inside, the prize possessions are the television and VCR. Wealthy families have several servants who sleep out in the courtyard, while the family sleeps inside.

Northern Sudanese villagers also live an Arab lifestyle, with thick-walled, square houses built around a central courtyard. Most villages are located on the banks of the Nile or at desert oases. Similar to life in the cities, village life occurs mostly outside during the day, in courtyards and at roadside tea-shops. People work in the fields, tend their animals, and make goods for sale or barter.

Collecting water and firewood are important chores in the village.

NOMADIC LIFE

More than a tenth of the population of Sudan have a nomadic or seminomadic existence.

Different nomadic groups have different ways of life. The Rasheida in eastern Sudan make their tents out of woven goat hair, while the nearby Hadebdowa tribe make their tents out of palm fiber mats.

Many northern tribes herd livestock such as cattle, goats, and camels, and wander the desert following the sudden rainstorms. After the storm

THE *SOUK*

All Sudanese towns have a marketplace known as the *souk*. It is usually the center of town both physically and socially. The *souk* is often a warren of streets in which it is easy to become lost.

The *souk* is divided into craft and merchandise sections—all the goldsmiths are in one part of the *souk*, while all the greengrocers are in another. The goldsmith makes jewelry in the back of the shop to sell at the front. Baskets and leather bags are sold here for daily use. Some *souks* sell only Western luxury items; others sell camels or donkeys. Throughout the *souk* are tea shops where hot, sweet mint tea can be drunk at one's leisure. These are popular places to meet friends and catch up on news and gossip.

a patch of desert that has been infertile for years suddenly blossoms and provides a temporary pasture for the vast herds of animals.

Other nomads are traders who make long journeys back and forth across the desert using camel trains, bartering gold or salt for other goods.

Nomads may drive their animals hundreds of miles across harsh terrain.

BROKEN FAMILIES

The disruption in the traditional patterns of life in Sudan by war, floods, droughts, and famine has resulted in the break-up of traditional family units. Many men have had to leave their families and go in search of work, leaving Muslim women as head of the household for the first time in their lives. The women have little or no means of income.

Sons also leave home at a very young age so as not to be a burden to their families. They go to the cities where they quickly become beggars and thieves, sleeping in the streets and often receiving injuries in street accidents. In Khartoum and Nyala there are programs to rehabilitate such children. They are taught a trade and encouraged to return to their homes.

A Dinka wedding dance. The cattle are being given as dowry.

LIFE IN THE SOUTH

As one travels farther south both the countryside and the people change. The indigenous population is black African rather than Arab, and their lifestyle has little in common with their northern compatriots. People wear fewer clothes and many decorate their bodies with scars.

The typical square, mud-brick houses give way to groups of round houses with mud walls and thatched straw roofs. The houses are arranged in circles around a swept, earthen courtyard where most of the village activities take place. Cooking is done over an open fire. The villages are often surrounded by grass walls to keep children inside and wildlife out.

Beyond the houses are small fields irrigated once a year by the Nile floods. In the floodplain as many as three harvests a year can be made. Most families work to produce their own food and enough to barter for their other needs. There are few paid jobs except for agricultural workers at harvest time.

Away from the floodplains people depend on wells for water. The government has dug many wells and provided a complex series of irrigation canals. In recent years, because of the drain on Sudan's water resources, wells have to be dug deeper and deeper before water is found.

South of the Sudd the dependence on the river for irrigation stops and the land is hot and verdant. Evidence of Western missionaries can be seen in the many clapboard churches and schools. The local people grow vegetables to sell in the north, keep cattle, and hunt game for food.

In more wooded and higher regions, houses are built with a structure of wood. People wear clothes to keep warm in the lower temperatures and fires are used for heating as well as cooking.

The war has brought huge disruption to the lives of many southerners, with whole tribes being displaced by raids from both sides.

Missionary institutions and other foreign aid organizations have been involved in the effort to distribute food to the war-torn south. This aid has now been banned by Bashir's government.

WOMEN

Arab women are very carefully guarded by their families. They do not mix socially with men, and they cover themselves with long cloths when they go outside. Women tend to spend much more time in the home, while men take care of business outside the home (including doing the daily shopping). There are few Arab girls living on the streets in Sudan; no matter how poor a family is, it is a tenet of their faith that girls are weak and should be protected, and even very distant cousins will be taken in if they have no other means of support.

Girls go through their exercises at a school in Khartoum.

SELF-HELP FOR WOMEN

In rural areas much of the daily grind of finding, growing, and preparing food is done by women. Aid agencies have become aware of the important role that women play in the survival of families and have begun to educate women and make use of their skills.

The Milebeda grinding mill is an example of this type of development. In 1993 a women's group called Yed el Marra, or Women's Fist, set up a grain mill in a remote village in south Darfur. In villages like this, women spend much of the day grinding grain by hand or carrying it to the nearest town to be ground. After being trained to operate the new mill, they found that they saved time and money and could even earn a little money grinding grain for other villages. The small profits go toward local literacy and health projects. The mill is run by simple, easily-replaced technology, so it does not depend on foreign technical help. More mills and training programs have been set up in other rural communities.

A girl is often married as a teenager to a man she might only have met a few times and may never have spoken to privately. Her husband pays a high bride price to her parents.

Because women are not allowed to attend school once they are married, few women have a college education. However, some girls are able to keep their marriage a secret and with the support of their husband can go on to further education.

Many non-Arab women live a very different lifestyle. They work hard in the fields, collecting water, caring for animals, and making goods to sell. The Felata tribe, south of Khartoum, believe that women should earn their own living. The girls are independent and many work, selling sweetmeats in the marketplaces. They wear brightly colored clothes and jewelry. Those who get the opportunity will attend school wearing shorts just like the boys in their class.

A MUSLIM WEDDING

A traditional Sudanese Muslim wedding lasts about three days. Once it would have lasted up to 40 days, but that custom is no longer followed. Before the married pair are betrothed, a good deal of bargaining goes on between the families of the bride and groom. The groom must pay a bride price to the bride's father in addition to bestowing a dowry on the bride herself.

As the wedding approaches it is customary for the girl to affect unhappiness. She may stop eating and look sad. Her body is oiled and perfumed, and all body hair except that on her head is removed using boiled sugar and lemon juice. Her hands are painted with henna in intricate curling patterns.

The night before the wedding, the groom holds a party in the courtyard. A feast is set out and men and women sit in separate groups to eat. After the food come speeches and dancing. The men dance first, in swaying, stamping rows. The women dance in groups of two or three, joining and stopping while the men dance continuously. While the dancing goes on, the groom walks around the groups of people waving a stick and shouting; the others shout back or howl at him.

The ceremony itself is carried out the following day by an *imam* (Muslim priest) in the presence of the parents. The bride and groom do not take part. Seven women go down to the Nile and throw food in, returning with water to wash the bride's face. That night the bride's family hold another party. The bride dances for the groom (pictured below, at a wedding in Omdurman), and he reaches under her skirt to cut the thongs of her undergarment.

HEALTH

Early in the 20th century the Sudanese people suffered from frequent epidemics of diseases such as meningitis, sleeping sickness, and yellow fever. The efforts of the Sudan Medical Service (later the Ministry of Health) and missionary institutions reduced the death rate, but in the 1980s and 1990s drought and war have resulted in a very low life expectancy. War, famine, and disease are the major causes of death, and life expectancy is only 46 years for men and 49 years for women. Infant mortality is around 100 deaths per thousand live births.

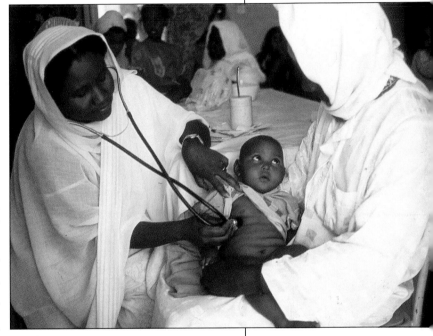

A man brings his child to a doctor at Khartoum Hospital.

There are about 160 hospitals in Sudan, most of them in the cities, with roughly one bed per 1,110 people. Hospital services are free. There are also doctors in private practice in the larger towns.

In rural areas and the south, medical care is very basic. There is a severe shortage of local doctors, so most medical care is undertaken by foreign aid workers and midwives with very basic training. Medical aid to the south has currently been suspended.

Only 46% of the population have access to safe water, so many people die of easily preventable diseases such as measles and dysentery. Tropical diseases such as malaria, river blindness, and tuberculosis are endemic in the Nile valley.

Due to a shortage of teachers and facilities, there are many children in each class.

In 1991, two years of Islamic education became compulsory for every student. Christian and other religious education was banned.

EDUCATION

Sudan technically provides six years of free compulsory education from ages 7 to 13, but in reality many rural children and displaced children have no schools to attend. Less than half of Sudan's children attend during the "compulsory" years. By the age of 13 only 13% attend school, and only 2% are educated beyond the age of 18. Girls make up less than 40% of school students. Although these figures are low, they are an improvement on previous generations: only 9% of people over 35 have any education at all.

There are three levels of schools: primary (7–12 years), intermediate (13–15 years), and secondary (15–18 years). The school year runs from July to March.

Sudan has three universities, in Khartoum, Omdurman, and Juba, and a teacher training college in Khartoum. Men wishing to go to university must first complete two years of service in the government militia.

FAMINE

For the past decade the lifestyle of many Sudanese has been dominated by the need to find food.

In 1985–1986 the west of Sudan around Kordofan and Darfur and the east near Kassala experienced unprecedented droughts. Four hundred thousand people from Kordofan came to central Sudan in search of food and water for their animals. Seven million people suffered from malnutrition and came close to starvation, and many died. The problem was made worse by temperatures of 126°F (52°C) and ferocious sandstorms.

A second wave of famine, this time caused by the war, hit Sudan in 1989. By this time a relief infrastructure was set up in Sudan with various aid agencies supplying food, but both the government and the SPLA caused problems, neither side wanting the other to receive the aid. Much of the aid went to government troops rather than the citizens of north or south Sudan.

An American journalist, Raymond Bonner, visited Sudan and described what he found. In one small village in southwest Sudan he was told that 50 children died each day. The relief workers did not have the facilities to bury them and their bodies were taken by scavenging animals. Ten thousand people were thought to have died in that one town. Meanwhile the local military garrison had food and medicine.

A villager in Kordofan uses a thumbprint to sign for sorghum.

RELIGION

SEVENTY PERCENT OF SUDAN'S POPULATION are Muslim, 25% practice many different indigenous religions, and 5% are Christian.

ISLAM

The word *Islam* means submission. Muslims believe in the word of God and submit to all his words as handed down by the prophets. Islam acknowledges as prophets several figures out of Christianity and Judaism, such as Abraham (Ibrahim), Adam, Noah, Moses, and Jesus. Muslims believe that Jesus is merely one of the prophets who have heard the word of God, rather than the son of God.

The most recent and revered of the prophets is Mohammed (A.D. 507–632). His following grew until after his death most of Arabia had converted to Islam. Mohammed's birthplace, Mecca in Saudi Arabia, became the religion's holy city because it was there that the first mosque was built. It is called the Kaaba and contains a black stone believed to have been given to Ibrahim by the Archangel Gabriel. Mohammed's words were collected into a holy book called the Koran (or Qur'an).

The third pillar of faith is to give one 17th of one's income to the poor. In Sudan, like most other Arab countries, this is no longer an enforced law but is left to the conscience of the individual.

THE FIVE PILLARS OF FAITH

Muslims must carry out five acts of faith. They must:

1. Publicly declare that there is no God but Allah and that Mohammed is his prophet.
2. Pray at sunrise, noon, mid-afternoon, sunset, and night.
3. Give alms to the poor.
4. Fast during the month of Ramadan.
5. Make a pilgrimage to Mecca at least once during their life.

Devout Muslims pray five times a day, even when at work.

ISLAMIC WORSHIP Muslims make a commitment to pray five times a day. At each of the prayer times the *muezzin* ("MU-ez-in") calls the faithful to the mosque. Before praying the devotee removes his or her shoes and holds them in the left hand. The body is carefully washed according to ritual and in a certain order. The devotee faces the direction of Mecca and goes through a ritual of standing, bowing, and sitting—reciting prescribed prayers as he or she does so. The prayers should be carried out in congregation, but if people cannot attend a mosque they can say their prayers alone. On Fridays there are special prayers in all mosques.

FASTING Fasting is required of all Muslims during the month of Ramadan. They must refrain from eating, drinking, smoking, and sexual activity from dawn to sunset. In addition, if they can afford it they must feed one poor person. The fast can be delayed if one is sick or on a hazardous journey.

PILGRIMAGE Every Muslim is obligated to make the journey to Mecca once in their lifetime. For thousands of Arab people that once meant a vast journey of several months across the Libyan and Nubian deserts in a camel train. The pilgrimage must be made in a state of grace, wearing a seamless white garment. The pilgrims must not cut their hair or nails or shed blood.

The Egyptian Mosque in Khartoum is one of Sudan's most famous landmarks.

ISLAMIC LAW Islamic law includes both legal and moral concepts. Many of the rules of Islamic law cannot be put into a legal system and must be a matter of conscience.

The laws of Islam are laid down in the Koran and another book called the Sunna, and have been added to by various religious groups over many centuries. They uphold the importance of the family and declare men and women to be equal, except that men are "a degree higher." The Koran forbids infanticide of girls, which was once common among the Arab tribes, allocates a degree of inheritance to girls, and describes the treatment of wives. Women are given the right of divorce in case of ill-treatment, but adultery is proscribed with a punishment of 100 lashes. Under Islamic law men are allowed to marry up to four wives and can divorce any wife at will. Other important laws of Islam forbid eating pork and drinking alcohol.

JIHAD This is usually translated to mean holy war. The Islamic goal is to "reform the earth." This is usually taken to mean the assumption of political power by Muslims in order to bring about Islamic law, and on occasion Muslim leaders have considered violence a reasonable means of achieving this. Just like Christians, the Muslims have used this idea as an excuse to invade other countries.

Pilgrims waiting to depart for Mecca.

ANIMISM

Animist religions are the most ancient religions practiced in Sudan. Animists believe that the natural objects around them have power and are able to influence their lives in many ways. Many animist groups worship one particular totem such as a wild animal, particular tree, or river and will do anything to avoid injuring that object.

Most animist tribes worship their ancestors, believing that the spirits of their ancestors must be carefully looked after because they have the power to bring harm or good to the family. Because each group respects the rights of other groups to worship their own ancestors, the various animist religions have never been in conflict, although the tribespeople have fought for other reasons.

Many people also believe in the evil eye. A bad look from another person with magical power or the help of a witch could cause them harm. They wear amulets to protect them from this, and small babies are kept well away from public view in case someone sees them and puts the evil eye on them.

Muslim and local religious traditions coexist among the Fur people. They splash sanctuaries with flour and water paste to ensure fertility and make sacrifices at shrines when the rains are likely to fall. The office of rainmaker is hereditary.

SHILLUK ANIMISM

The Shilluk tribe believes in a supreme creator called Juok. Another of their most important gods is Nyikang, who they believe created the Shilluk nation and brings the rain that revives people after the long dry season. Nyikang encompasses the three main divisions of their universe—earth, sky, and water—the only elements they know in the savannah where there are no mountains or forests. The Shilluk also worship their ancestors and believe that spirits live in the trees and plants around them. They believe that the river holds herds of ghost animals, which are tended by the spirits in the bush.

TRIBAL MEDICINE

The aid groups who have gone to Sudan to help with the refugee crises, famines, and floods record some of the local beliefs, especially those concerning medicine. One traditional cure for certain illnesses is to burn the victim with hot nails to drive out the illness, while a cure for malaria is to make 44 cuts on the patient's body. The Fallata Umboro tribe in western Sudan has teachers called *faki* ("FAY-ki") who are part teacher and part magician. For one month each year the *faki* collect herbs and roots that they make into spells and potions to cure illnesses or arouse the interest of a potential lover.

Many southern tribespeople call on traditional doctors in times of sickness or hardship.

CHRISTIANITY

Nubia was a Christian kingdom for centuries before the advent of Islam. Many religious orders are still active in Sudan, although the kind of evangelical Christianity that has taken hold in much of the rest of Africa is not so prevalent here. Most of Sudan's Catholics are in the south. Great cathedrals built by missionaries still exist, and there are still missions operating schools and hospitals in the south. The rhythms of African music have influenced religious meetings all over the country.

An outdoor church service in southern Sudan.

LANGUAGE

THERE ARE MORE THAN 100 LANGUAGES spoken in Sudan. Many of these languages are spoken by quite tiny numbers of people.

The main language is a form of Arabic that is spoken throughout the country. Arabic began its rise to prominence in the 14th century, and its position was established when it was made the official language of government of the Funj sheikhdom, the Mahdist state, and early colonial governments. In the south the language of the Dinka people is a lingua franca (common language) used between local tribespeople. English once had an official role in the country and many people still speak it, especially in the south where English missionaries established schools.

Most Sudanese speak at least two or three languages: their own mother tongue, Arabic, and some English, as well as a smattering of other tribal languages.

THE LANGUAGE OF ANCIENT MEROË

A written language existed in ancient Sudan since the third millennium B.C. Egyptian rulers left inscriptions on their tombs in Sudan written in Egyptian hieroglyphics. The black African civilization that created the city of Meroë had its own written script, which was completely unrelated to ancient Egyptian. It is so dissimilar that many of the inscriptions found at Meroë have not yet been deciphered. Rather than a series of hieroglyphs like ancient Egyptian, the written language of Meroë used a cursive alphabet.

ARABIC

Arabic is the major language in Sudan, spoken either as a mother tongue or as a lingua franca between groups of other language speakers. The standard form of Arabic from Saudi Arabia is the official language and is used in official documents and on formal occasions. However, very few people understand it or use it well. This causes serious educational problems, since it is the official language of education and the language in which textbooks are printed.

Most urban residents, pastoralists and farmers in the north and center of the country speak a unique form of Arabic that has developed in Sudan. It is mutually intelligible to some extent with Egyptian Arabic, but has some differences. Sudanese Arabic is spoken by 15 million people in Sudan and is the language of trade.

In this village with no classroom, Arabic is taught outside under a shady tree.

In the south a creole or pidgin language has developed. This creole is similar to Sudanese Arabic but could not be understood by an Egyptian. It is the first language of about 20,000 people in the area around Juba and south into Equatoria, and about 44,000 people speak it as their second language. It replaces Arabic as the lingua franca in the far south. It is the language of trade and the language that many schoolteachers use unofficially in the classroom.

The three forms of Arabic used in Sudan are only partly mutually intelligible, in the same way that Spanish and Portuguese speakers can understand a little of what a speaker of the other language is saying. All three forms of the language are tonal, which means that they use intonation to change the meaning of a word. The same group of letters said in a different tone has a completely different meaning.

WRITTEN ARABIC

Arabic script, written from right to left, is based on a different system from that of the Roman alphabet. The Roman alphabet is not able to describe all the sounds in Arabic, nor can it represent the tones. Written Arabic is difficult for Sudanese to learn because Sudanese Arabic is so different from the standard form. Some Sudanese Arabic words cannot be represented in Arabic script, while some Arabic script does not represent the actual words used by Sudanese Arabic speakers, let alone Creole speakers.

The number of people who use Creole Arabic as a first or second language is increasing all the time at the expense of English, which is gradually going out of use.

GREETINGS AND BODY LANGUAGE

When greeting someone in Arabic, it is common to touch one's heart and say "Salaam aleyakum" ("sah-LAHM ah-LAY-ah-koom"—Peace be with you), followed by "Kayf halak" ("KYFE hah-LAHK"—How are you?).

The right hand is held out in a formal handshake between strangers, although a man will never touch a woman unless the woman offers her hand first. Often men will embrace each other in a hug on greeting, but men and women rarely embrace in this way.

As in many other Muslim countries, use of the left hand is avoided as much as possible. Objects are passed between people with either the right hand or with both hands, never the left only. Pointing at someone with the left hand would also be considered improper.

The Beja, a Muslim nomadic tribe living in the Red Sea Hills, speak Bedawiya, a language that has no written form. It is spoken by about 150,000 people.

Opposite: **Missionary institutions taught English and recorded African tribal languages.**

AFRICAN LANGUAGES

There are about a hundred different African languages spoken in Sudan. They can be classified into groups based on certain similarities in grammar and structure but are mostly mutually incomprehensible. This gives us some indication of just how ancient African society is. The more unlike two languages from the same language family are, the longer the two must have been spoken in order for such differences to have evolved.

The 1,000 different languages of Africa are divided into four major groups. Arabic belongs to one of those groups, the Hamito-Semitic family. Some of the languages spoken along the Red Sea coast of Sudan are also members of this language family.

Most of the African languages spoken in Sudan belong to a completely different group, the Nilo-Saharan family. Some of these languages are mutually intelligible. For example, the language spoken by the Fur people around Darfur is spoken by only 70,000 people but can be understood by speakers of Nyala, Laguri, and other languages spoken in the area.

The most widely spoken non-Arabic language is Dinka, which is spoken in the south as a mother tongue and as a lingua franca. Dinka is spoken by about two million people and in certain areas is used unofficially in classrooms. It has wide regional differences, but can be understood by the Shilluk, who have their own language and live as far north as Khartoum.

Like most things in Sudan, language has become a political issue. As part of the government drive to Islamicize Sudan, great emphasis has been placed on the acquisition of Arabic. Most speakers of Arabic as a mother tongue are Muslim. Although some Muslim tribes speak their own tribal mother tongue, they also use Arabic, and the indigenous languages are expected to decline.

In the south and in the Nuba Mountains, refusing to speak Arabic is a means of resistance. The Nuba, who have been under intense pressure to abandon their culture, have chosen to teach their own languages in their schools. The Nuba, and many organizations such as Amnesty International, believe that their very existence is under threat, and speaking Nuba languages is one way of ensuring their survival until better times.

LITERACY

Literacy classes teach reading and writing skills to adults who missed out on early schooling.

Sudan has poor literacy levels. Only 45% of men and 18% of women are able to read. With its hundreds of mother tongues, Sudan has had many problems in improving the rate of literacy. This was made worse by the changeover in the 1970s from English to Arabic as the medium of instruction.

THE MEDIA

The media has had a difficult time in Sudan as each successive coup has changed the direction of government. In 1970 all privately owned newspapers were nationalized. There are two daily newspapers in Arabic: *El Ayam* ("EL EYE-ahm") and *El Sahafa* ("EL sah-HAH-fah"). A four-page daily English language newspaper called the *Sudan Times* is published in Khartoum, and the *Nile Mirror*, an English weekly newspaper, is published in Juba. The state also produces an English magazine called *Sudanow*.

Less than 5% of the population reads a daily newspaper. This figure is a reflection of literacy levels rather than indifference to the news. Radio is a more common medium. About 75 people in a thousand own a radio, and many people have access to one for at least part of the day. The broadcasting company is state-owned, but people can also tune in to the Voice of America and the BBC World Service.

Television is a rare luxury owned by the wealthy few and by some of the richer social clubs. The one television station is government-owned. Over 60% of television programs are produced locally, and a typical night's viewing contains news broadcasts, farming information, religious programs, commercials, and lastly entertainment, which makes up about half the broadcasting time.

There are about six books in Sudan for every one thousand people.

A bookshop in Khartoum.

ARTS

SUDAN HAS BEEN HOME to civilized life for thousands of years. Its cultural heritage goes back to the civilizations of ancient Egypt and Meroë, which produced complex architecture and artwork. At Musawwarat es Sufra is an interesting excavation of a huge Meroitian building with long, wide corridors, ramps, mazes, and rooms for which no one has discovered a purpose. One archeologist has suggested that it was used for training elephants! In more modern times great cathedrals and mosques have been built as an expression of the spiritual nature of the people of Sudan.

Sudan has also produced musicians and artists from both its African and Arabic traditions. Khartoum has a college of fine arts whose students often put on displays of their work. That such institutions are still operating in Sudan is a sign of hope for the country.

Opposite: **A Dinka potter uses a piece of grass to make a pattern in wet clay.**

LIBRARIES AND MUSEUMS

Sudan has about 10 major libraries, the largest of which is Khartoum University Library with around 90,000 volumes. There are five museums, most of them in Khartoum. The National Museum, in the center of the city, has two floors depicting the ancient history of Sudan, with displays of the remains of ancient Kush and Nubia and rescued frescoes from the early churches. In the garden of the museum are reconstructed temples of Buhen and Semna, salvaged during the construction of the Aswan Dam. The Temple of Buhen dates back to 1490 B.C. and was built by the Egyptian Queen Hatshepsut. Another museum in the city is dedicated to artifacts of village life, many of them still in use.

Small pyramids held the bodies of Meroitian rulers.

ANCIENT ART AND ARCHITECTURE

One of the earliest sites of ancient architecture is at Meroë, on the east bank of the Nile north of Khartoum. Meroë is represented by many sites, including the luxurious Royal City, dating back to the fourth century B.C., which is built inside an area of about 0.4 square miles (1 square km). It is a walled city, within which is another walled area, believed to be the palace. The buildings, which are of mud brick and often faced with fired and glazed bricks, included palaces, audience chambers, and temples. Most interesting though was an ornately decorated swimming pool with a complex set of water channels bringing water into it from a nearby well.

Iron objects and pottery of a high quality have been found at many sites. The pottery was thrown on a potter's wheel, fired, and decorated. Many of them are considered the finest pottery objects found in Africa. Remains of textiles prove that cotton was grown and made into cloth here at a very early stage.

EARLY CHRISTIAN ART AND ARCHITECTURE

Christian culture dominated the Middle Nile from about the sixth century A.D. Northern Sudan had several major cities where commercial, political, and social life were highly complex and structured. Many churches were in good condition when they were abandoned, and over the centuries they have filled with windblown sand. The remains of three cathedrals and at least 100 churches dating from the fourth century to the 15th century have been found. The earlier buildings are bigger and grander than later ones, suggesting that Christianity declined over this period.

Churches built by the Coptic sect had huge stone supporting columns and brick-lined vaults. There are remains of cathedrals at Old Dongola, Faras, and Qasr Ibrim. In the cathedral at Faras wall paintings of a high artistic quality have been preserved in the desert for hundreds of years. The paintings depict Biblical scenes, Nubian kings, and high government officials.

In some sites gold and glass lamps have been discovered, along with gold and silver jewelry set with precious stones. Further evidence indicates that gold and architectural stone were mined or excavated in Sudan, and either worked in the country or traded abroad.

A detailed fresco (wall painting) from the ancient cathedral at Faras.

MODERN ARCHITECTURE

Just as in ancient times, architecture says much about the spiritual and aesthetic life of a country. Modern Sudan's architectural masterpieces are its cathedrals and mosques. In Khartoum the most interesting mosque is

The distinctive dome of the Mosque of Two Niles in Khartoum.

the modern Two Niles Mosque, which stands at the confluence of the Blue Nile and the White Nile. Opened in 1984, it is a huge dome-shaped geometrical building, standing out stark and white against the browns and reds of the desert. Conical patterns around its base remind the observer of the many memorials to holy men that are scattered throughout the country. Another Khartoum mosque, built by King Farouk of Egypt, reflects a very different, almost colonial, style of architecture. Its minaret and walls are ornately carved stone more in keeping with the architecture of colonial Khartoum.

At El Obeid is a large Catholic cathedral in which many aspects of African culture come together. Smaller churches are much simpler in design and more in keeping with African architecture. They are simple wooden or mud-walled buildings with straw roofs, which like most African architecture will eventually disappear, leaving no evidence of their existence.

ARTS AND CRAFTS

Craftwork is still an important element in daily Sudanese life. In the West crafts have become an expensive rarity, but in Sudan quite everyday objects are handmade using ancient techniques. Domestic objects are woven using palm leaves or grasses, and complex woodcarving is still in evidence. In Port Sudan, now quite rundown since Sudanese exports have declined, the older buildings still display elegant lattice work in their window frames and doorways. In nearby Suakin the crumbling buildings show elegant architecture made from coral stone, which is gradually being eroded by the desert winds.

Craftsworkers producing objects in gold, silver, and brass can be found in any *souk* in Sudan. Some tribes wear exquisite silver and gold jewelry or carry ornate decorative swords, daggers, and knives, all of which can be seen being made in the marketplace. Elaborate leather goods are made by the nomadic tribes to barter for food. Many of the southern tribes wear ornate necklaces made from ivory and precious stones. For the almost-defunct tourist industry there are many carvings in ebony and other precious woods.

LITERATURE

Sudan has an ancient tradition of storytelling. Some stories told around firesides in Sudan have existed in one form or another for centuries. Many of the languages of Sudan had no written form until the missionaries began to transcribe them, so history and traditions were handed down from one generation to another in an oral tradition.

In modern times men and women have found a voice in Sudanese society, relating some of the ancient tales and making new ones to record the lifestyles of the Sudanese. One modern Sudanese writer is Tayeb Saleh who writes fictionalized accounts of the life of Sudanese people. His novels include *The Wedding of Zein and other Stories* and *The Season of Migration to the North*, both published in Washington, D.C. in 1978.

MUSIC

The people of Africa have made use of percussion and string instruments as part of their religious worship and daily life for centuries, and Sudan is no exception. Many different types of percussion instruments can be heard at religious celebrations and tribal dances.

The Dinka record all their activities, especially war, initiation, and other major life events, in song. Through their songs the people can reinforce their identity, recall their ancestors, praise their group, or settle a dispute. Since they enshrine the history, beliefs, and values of the Dinka, many songs are about their all-important cattle.

The popular music of the north is influenced by the sounds, language, and instruments of Arabic culture. Khartoum and Omdurman have recording facilities that are accessible to rising talents as well as established masters, and the wealth of popular music is disseminated through radio and inexpensive cassettes.

The oud *("OOD") is a musical instrument dating back to at least the seventh century. It is the most important musical instrument in Arab culture and is regarded as the forerunner of the European lute. It usually has five strings and is played with a plectrum or with the fingers of both hands.*

A vibrantly decorated six-stringed tambour.

THREE MODERN SUDANESE MUSICIANS

Abdel Gadir Salim, Abdel Aziz El Mubarak, and Mohamed Gubara are popular Sudanese musicians whose music has been brought to the West through albums and performances.

Salim fronts a small ensemble of *oud*, *tabla* (a kind of drum), and accordion, highlighting the rhythms and melodies and the voice of the artist. He also plays with a larger band.

Mubarak sings with *oud*, drum, and accordion. His influences are broader than Salim's with traces of many other cultures slipping into his more urban interpretation.

Gubara plays with a tambour. His sharper vocal style and sparse accompaniment create stunning music with an almost chilling intensity and energy.

LEISURE

WAR, FAMINE, AND POVERTY have hit some areas of Sudan harder than others, so the opportunity for leisure varies. In some areas life goes on pretty much as it always has. In the bigger towns and cities the morning is spent working, while the afternoons are usually a time for resting until it is cooler. In the evenings, after offices close at 8 pm, most men relax in one of the many clubs organized by religious, trade, or tribal associations. The clubs usually serve food and nonalcoholic drinks, provide lectures or sporting activities such as squash, and occasionally have a television set or even show a movie. Card games are also popular.

Attending a club is less common for women. Women usually stay at home in the evening, prepare the evening meal, and perhaps, if they are wealthy, watch some television.

Opposite: **Refugees in a Sudanese camp play a game with stones.**

Left: **Even in harsh times, children still find ways to have fun.**

DAILY LEISURE

Outside the clubs, most towns are empty, dark places after sundown. There are very few restaurants, no street lighting, and most of the nightlife activities common in the West are disapproved of. This was not the case before the declaration of shariah law. Khartoum had a reputation as a fast town where all kinds of nightlife went on and bars sold local and imported alcohol. There are still illegal drinking clubs selling home-brewed and distilled drinks.

One of the most popular leisure activities in Sudan is simply resting in the shade, drinking tea and talking with friends.

In the long hot afternoons, for those who do not sleep, there are many tea shops to visit to hear the latest gossip or to read the daily paper. In many societies shopping has become a leisure activity. To some extent this is true in Sudan, but instead of shopping malls there is the *souk*, which is liveliest in the early morning, and where mostly men or older women go to do each day's shopping. In some towns there will be newly arrived groups of nomads with gossip from their last port of call or new shipments of scarce goods to go and look over.

SPORTS

A very popular sport in Sudan is football (soccer) of the kind played in Europe. There is a national league, and some towns have two or more teams. El Obeid often tops the football league. Where there is a television European matches are watched avidly.

Wrestling is a traditional pastime among the Dinka.

Wrestling is a famous tradition among the Nuba. This activity contributed to the Nuba's problems when it became a major tourist attraction in the 1970s and early 1980s. The Muslim government decided that the naked wrestling and dancing was irreligious, and the campaign to clothe and "civilize" the Nuba began.

Sudan has always been a country where fine horses are bred, and Khartoum has a racecourse that is patronized by many of its citizens. Races are held on Fridays and Sundays and polo matches are held on Wednesdays and Saturdays.

Besides their passion for football, most Sudanese have little time or money for sports. Some sports are organized in expatriate settlements that spring up as groups of aid workers arrive. A team building a road from El Obeid has a swimming pool, and some settlements have table tennis and other activities to keep the workers occupied. The expatriate community is biggest in Khartoum and is organized around national clubs.

Small boys play football in bare patches, even in the desert, all over Sudan.

A group of Dinka children entertain themselves.

CHILDREN

Children in the West have a lot of leisure time, but for many Sudanese children games have to take second place to survival. Most rural children work alongside their mothers in the fields if they are not in school, and many spend a large part of each day traveling to and from the nearest source of water. Children as young as 5 are left in charge of their younger brothers and sisters. The children of the Dinka tribe spend their days in charge of their animals. When children do have leisure time it is spent perhaps in finding a use for pieces of scrap metal, bending them into the shapes of toys to sell to other people, or making kites from sticks and old plastic welded together with a burning cigarette.

STORYTELLING

One traditional activity that survives in Sudan is storytelling. Stories are passed on from older generations to the young. The Sudanese of the south share many of the folk stories of other areas of Africa, such as the stories of Ananse the spider man—a story that also came to America with the Africans taken into slavery in the 18th and 19th centuries.

Other stories concern ghosts or history. In eastern Sudan there is a town called Suakin, which means "land of the genie." Suakin was said to be the home of a powerful genie. One legend tells how the queen of one of the tribes of the Yemen sent a ship carrying seven virgin girls to King Solomon in Jerusalem. When the ship arrived in Jerusalem all the girls were expecting babies. The ship had been driven to Suakin by a storm, and all the girls had had affairs with the genie!

The Sudanese have lots of ghost stories to tell. One modern story tells of a tree that was used to hang criminals outside an old prison in Kassala. Local people believed that the suffering spirits of those executed lived in the tree. The tree died and was cut down to be used for firewood, but no one in the village would touch it. When a passing traveler took some of the wood and lit a fire he heard the voices of the dead people calling out to him from the flames.

There are about 60 movie theaters in Sudan, mostly in the towns. About 2.8 million people go to the movies each year. All films are imported from other countries, about half of them coming from the United States.

FESTIVALS

DESPITE THEIR HARDSHIPS, people continue celebrating the important festivals of their lives. Sudan has three major religious groups: Muslim, Christian, and animist. The major Muslim festivals and Christmas Day coincide with public holidays. Other major public holidays are January 1, which celebrates Sudanese Independence, and March 27; ironically, this holiday commemorates the signing of the peace agreement between the SPLA and the government in 1972, which has been broken many times.

MUSLIM FESTIVALS

There are two major religious festivals for Sudanese Muslims: Eid el-Fitr, which marks the end of Ramadan, and Eid el-Adha, which commemorates Abraham being asked to sacrifice his son. Another day that many children look forward to is the Prophet Mohammed's birthday.

Opposite: **Dinka dancing in southern Sudan.**

Left: **Music plays an important part in many Sudanese festivals.**

A colorfully dressed member of the Muslim Dervish sect celebrates in the streets of Sudan.

THE ISLAMIC CALENDAR

The calendar used in most of the world is known as the Gregorian calendar. It divides the year into a number of fixed days and months, with an extra day being added every four years (leap year) to allow for the difference between the calendar year of 365 days and the actual time it takes for the Earth to circle the Sun (which is just a little longer). Most Christian festivals, with the important exception of Easter, are based on this Gregorian solar calendar. Christmas Day is always December 25 and New Year's Day is always January 1.

Most Muslim festivals are based on the moon's rotation around the Earth, following a lunar calendar. There are still 12 months, of either 29 or 30 days, but the lunar year is therefore 10 or 11 days shorter than the Gregorian solar year. As a result, Muslim festivals are not held at the same time each year. The dates change each year; it takes 33 years for a complete cycle.

EID EL-FITR During Ramadan, the month of fasting, the breaking of the fast each day occurs at the moment of dusk. Each evening becomes a feast as the family settles down to enjoy the success of another day's fasting. Eid el-Fitr, on the first day of the 10th month, marks the end of Ramadan. Not surprisingly, it is characterized by feasting during the day. From a religious point of view, Eid el-Fitr signifies the glorious culmination of a period of spiritual cleansing and purification.

Eid el-Fitr is the most festive period of the year for Sudanese Muslims. It is celebrated with large family meals, which all members of an extended family will try to attend. Towards the end of Ramadan, the family home will be thoroughly cleaned in preparation. If there is money for new clothes or new furniture, this is the time when the shopping will be done. During the four days of celebration people wear their new clothes and visit friends and relatives. Eid el-Fitr is a cross between Thanksgiving and Christmas, being a religious, family, and social festival. Children receive gifts at this time of the year.

THE ZAR CEREMONY

Many women spend long periods of their life in the home, so festivals are often an occasion for women to go out and mix more freely than usual. The Zar ceremony is just such an opportunity. It is held to help women who are emotionally troubled. The ceremony is thought to soothe the spirits that possess them.

The highlight of the ceremony is a dance where women beat out a rhythm with drums and rattles, and troubled women get to their feet to dance to the music. A woman might have a particular object or talisman associated with the spirit that troubles her, and she will dance holding the object. The ceremony sometimes lasts as long as seven days.

THE ZIKR CEREMONY

This Muslim ceremony is regularly celebrated in the bigger towns of north Sudan. The men who take part in the ceremony are known as Whirling Dervishes. They believe that through the rhythm and movement of dance they can gain a state of rapture and so commune with God. The men, wearing long white *jallabiya* and turbans, meet near a holy place. The holy men who conduct the ceremony wear traditional colorful patched clothes.

Men move to the rhythm of drums, and from time to time one will break away from the crowd and whirl himself into a state of religious ecstasy. Young boys practice the dance at the outskirts of the crowd and the occasional woman may join in, much to the disapproval of the men. The ceremony takes place on Friday evenings as dusk approaches, and continues until night has fallen.

CHRISTIAN FESTIVALS

Once Christian festivals were an important part of daily life in Sudan, but as English influence wanes fewer people take part in them. Catholics celebrate the coming of Christmas with Midnight Mass. Christmas Day is a public holiday, so families in the city spend the day together. Christians give gifts and eat a special Christmas lunch—a Sudanese feast rather than the traditional Western lunch. Easter is also celebrated, although it is not a public holiday.

ANIMIST FESTIVALS

Animist festivals are usually associated with the cycles of nature, such as harvests, changes of the seasons, the rise and fall of the Nile, and the coming of rain. The Shilluk have two major festivals, the rain dance and the harvest festival. Both festivals involve dance and offerings to the ancestors. They and the Dinka also have fishing festivals where hundreds of men go into the river in the Sudd to catch as many fish as possible.

ANIMAL SACRIFICE

Many animist tribes practice animal sacrifice. To celebrate a special day (or to ward off danger or illness) the Dinka and Nuer tribes will kill one of their cattle. By performing the ritual they believe that a benevolent spiritual presence is brought to the occasion. The ritual sacrifice involves long speeches and many gestures with the spear, and when the animal is killed it is shared among the whole community according to strict laws of division. The ritual itself, rather than the killing of the animal, is most important; if the Nuer have no ox available, they will substitute a nonedible cucumber and perform the rites in exactly the same way, even calling the cucumber "ox."

FOOD

ALL TRAVELERS TO SUDAN agree that the Sudanese people, poor as they are, are among the most hospitable in the world. Travelers tell stories of how all over Sudan they were welcomed into people's homes and invited to share their food. In recent years Sudanese people have experienced the worst extremes of poverty and hardship and yet Sudanese hospitality remains the same.

Throughout Sudan an important dish is *ful* ("FOOL"), made of cooked beans and often served with raw onions. In villages along the Nile or along a truck route, there are more luxuries such as lentils and okra to add to the *ful*. Rice, sorghum, and millet are the staple grains. Sudanese eat flat Arabic bread and their own variety of bread called *kisra* ("KISS-rah"), a pancake-like unleavened bread made from sorghum.

Salt is a rare commodity and is bought in precious little packets from the market.

Opposite: **A woman stirs food for refugees at Mwehli camp.**

Left: **Flat bread, laid out ready for the oven, is one of the staple foods of northern Sudan.**

FRESH INGREDIENTS

In the desert regions vegetables and fresh fruit are a rare luxury, and *ful* with *kisra* may be the only things people eat for weeks on end. In the south, where it rains regularly, there are citrus fruits and many varieties of vegetables to make a varied and interesting diet.

Meat is a rarity all over Sudan, partly because livestock owners are reluctant to destroy the animals that represent their wealth, and partly because of the high cost and short storage life of meat. One way the Sudanese preserve meat is to dry it, cut it into strips and then grind it to a powder that is added to stews. Favorite meats are lamb and chicken. Many people eat fish caught from the Nile or the lakes in the mountains. Fish is often eaten for breakfast.

There is very little processed food or refrigeration, so most food is bought fresh daily from the *souk.* Certain things are only seasonally available.

Fresh vegetables are available at this market in Nyala.

ALCOHOL

Under shariah law alcohol is forbidden to all citizens of Sudan, but illegal brews are made in remote areas and enjoyed by many people. *Seiko* ("SAY-koh"), or *aragi* ("ah-rah-gi"), is distilled from dates and is a little like white rum. In other areas *tedj,* a wine made from dates, is preferred. A beer called *merissa* is brewed from sorghum. It is easily available in the south.

EATING HABITS

Most Sudanese start their day with a cup of very sweet milky tea called *shai bi nana* ("SHY bee NAH-nah"). All over the city and small towns and at intervals along all routes there are women with simple tea-making equipment ready to serve this breakfast delicacy.

The first meal of the day comes after the first of the morning's work at around 9:30. For the better-off this is often a dish with liver, such as cooked liver with *ful* and fish, or raw lungs and liver served with hot chili. A second meal is eaten in the evening and might be vegetable stew with *ful*, salad, and if the family can afford it, a piece of mutton or beef. In the evening a drink of hot sweetened milk called *laban* ("LAY-ban") is popular.

For many women whose husbands have been lost or have gone in search of work, brewing and selling alcohol is their only means of making a living.

Outdoor tea shops cater to travelers throughout Sudan. This one is at the bus station in Khartoum.

In Muslim households, the right hand is always used to give and receive food.

A SUDANESE FEAST

As the guests arrive they are offered a cooling drink such as freshly squeezed citrus juice, or *kakaday*, made from the hibiscus flower. The drinks are unsweetened so as not to spoil the palate.

After freshening up, the guests are taken to the dining room, which is decorated with peacock feathers. Men and women are served in separate rooms. At the center of the dining room is a low table surrounded by large comfortable cushions. A copper pitcher containing water and a large bowl are brought in, and guests' hands are washed.

The meal begins with soup brought out already served in bowls carried on a huge copper tray. Each guest is given a bowl, which is held in the left hand while a spoon is held in the right. When the guests have finished they return the bowl and spoon to the tray, which is then taken away.

The next tray carries the five or six remaining dishes of the meal, including *kisra* (flat bread), which is used to scoop up the sauces. The host will serve each person a piece of bread and a bowl of salad, and guests help themselves to food from the other dishes. Chili is served in little individual bowls. Food is eaten with spoons or with the right hand.

The hand-washing ritual is carried out again after the main course, and then dessert is served. There are very few cooked Sudanese desserts. Usually fresh fruit is peeled and served in segments, but there are a few more complicated dishes, such as *hashab* ("HASH-ab"), a dish made from chopped bananas, figs, and raisins. Another is very similar to crème caramel.

After the food, Jebbena coffee is served. This is named after the little cups in which it is served. If guests prefer, they can have *shai shada* ("SHY SHA-dah"), which is sweet hot tea spiced with cloves and cinnamon.

Finally the guests relax around the table while an incense burner filled with sandalwood is brought into the room to perfume the air.

A selection of Sudanese foods, including fried liver, *ful*, and bread.

THE FEAST MENU

For a very special occasion an animal will be slaughtered. The menu might be:
shorba – a soup made from pureed lamb; *maschi* – tomatoes and eggplant stuffed with rice and minced lamb; *gammonia* – stewed sheep's stomach, served with tomatoes and onions; salad of tomatoes, lettuce, onions, and green peppers with a lime-juice dressing; *shata* – a little bowl of hot chili to add to the dishes; *kisra*; fresh fruit segments; coffee.

A RECIPE FOR SHORBA
(PUREE OF LAMB KHARTOUM)

This interesting soup is a medium puree sparkled with peanut butter and lemon. The Sudanese usually add rice but it can be omitted. The amount of garlic can also be adjusted to taste.

(Serves 8)

3 lbs (1.4 kg) lamb bones
2 quarts water
2 tablespoons salt
1 cup onions (peeled and chopped)
1 cup carrots (peeled and cut in chunks)
1 cup cabbage (cut in small wedges)
1 cup string beans (trimmed)
3 cloves garlic (finely chopped)
4 tablespoons peanut butter
juice of one lemon
$^1/_2$ cup cooked rice (optional)
salt and pepper to taste

Place the lamb bones, water and salt in a large saucepan and simmer for one hour.

Add all the vegetables and garlic. Simmer for another hour until the vegetables are thoroughly cooked.

Remove the lamb bones and put the mixture through a sieve or food processor.

Add the peanut butter, thinned with the lemon juice.

Add the rice (optional).

Adjust the seasoning with salt and pepper.

Serve in soup bowls (one cup per portion).

In northern Sudan there is a very special way of brewing coffee, called Jebbena Sudanese. The coffee beans are fried over charcoal in a special pot and then ground with cloves and spices. The coffee is steeped in hot water, strained through a fresh grass sieve, and served in tiny coffee cups.

TABOOS

The Islamic rules regarding which foods are clean apply in Sudan, where the majority of people are Muslim. Pork is not eaten in Muslim households (except among the Nuba, who believe that it is acceptable to eat pork and also to drink alcohol). Muslim law also prohibits eating shellfish, but this is not commonly available in Sudan anyway.

Muslims eat only with the right hand, believing that the left hand is unclean.

During the month of Ramadan, breaking fast together at the end of the day is an important ritual for Muslim families.

KITCHENS AND UTENSILS

Because Sudan is one of the hottest countries in the world, most cooking takes place outside the house.

In more rural areas houses are one-room mud-walled huts with roofs of straw. Cooking is done outside over an open fire, which is often set in a hollow in the ground, with low mud walls built up the sides. Balanced on the mud walls is a huge wok-like metal pot on which the thick vegetable and meat stews are boiled. The fire is fuelled with wood kindling collected from the bush. Cooking utensils, spoons, cups, and plates are also made from natural products, such as gourds, large leaves, or wood from the date palm.

There is no running water—water is stored in animal skins or in oil drums to which wheels have been added to make the trips to the well easier. In some places the trunks of baobab trees are hollowed out and waterproofed with pitch to serve as water tanks.

Nomad cooking facilities are quite similar except that they are small enough to be packed away and moved. In the desert there is less firewood to be found, so cooking is done very carefully using animal dung as fuel. In many areas of

Beja girls cook sorghum porridge in the Red Sea province.

Sudan the ash from this type of fire is used as an effective mosquito repellent. Animal skins are used to store water and to make tents, and cooking implements may be made of bone. Rather than growing all their own food, the nomads must visit towns to barter goods for fresh vegetables and enough sorghum and beans to last until their next visit to a town.

City kitchens are a little more sophisticated, but most people still cook outdoors over charcoal stoves. Many dishes such as meat kebabs and grilled liver are cooked directly over the coals, like a Western barbecue. There is piped water in some areas, although it is generally untreated water piped straight from the river. People have to boil their drinking water to kill the parasites that live in it. Plastic and metal kitchen utensils are bought from the *souk*.

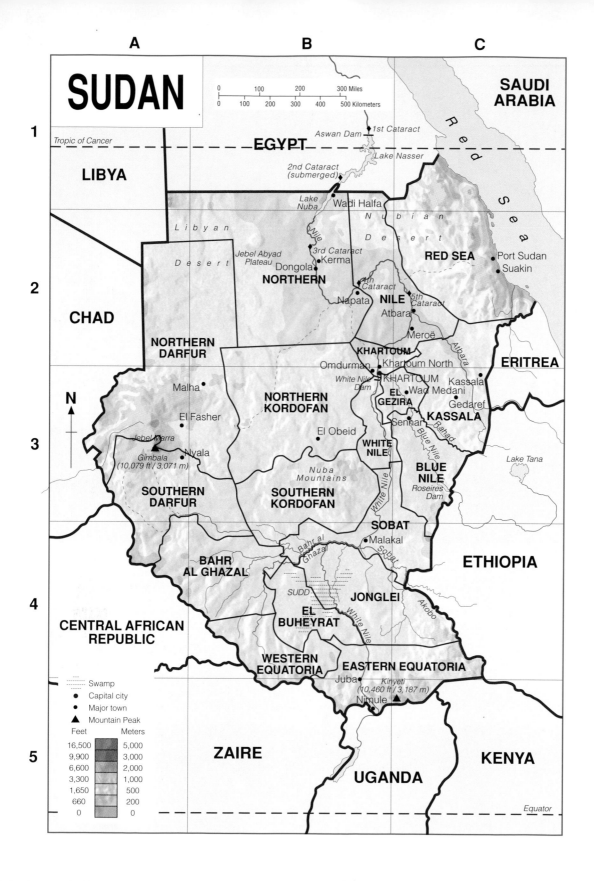

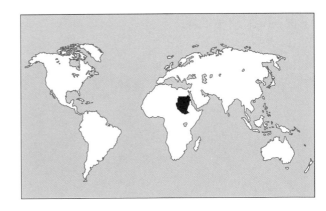

QUICK NOTES

OFFICIAL NAME
Democratic Republic of Sudan
(Jumhouriyyat es Sudan Democratiyya)

LAND AREA
967,494 square miles
2,505,809 square kilometers

CAPITAL
Khartoum

MAJOR TOWNS
Omdurman, Khartoum North, Port Sudan

MAJOR RIVERS
Blue Nile, White Nile, Atbara

HIGHEST POINT
Mt. Kinyeti, 10,460 feet (3,187 meters)

POPULATION
28.75 million

LIFE EXPECTANCY
Males: 46 years; females: 49 years

INFANT MORTALITY
112 deaths per 1,000 live births

CURRENCY
Sudanese pound (US$1 = 2 pounds)

RELIGION
70% Muslim, 25% Animist, 5% Christian.

MAJOR EXPORTS
Cotton, gum arabic, livestock.

MAJOR IMPORTS
Oil, wheat, agricultural machinery, foreign
aid, manufactured goods.

NATIONAL FLAG
Horizontal red, white, and black stripes, green
triangle at left.

NATIONAL SYMBOL
A lammergeier—desert vulture. Stylized wings
between two scrolls in Arabic. Upper one says
"Victory to Our Cause," the lower one gives the
name of the country.

NATIONAL DAY
Independence Day—January 1

IMPORTANT POLITICAL LEADERS
Muhammad Ahmad (the Mahdi), fought against
colonial rule in the 1880s–1890s.

Jaafar al-Nimeiry, president from 1969 to 1985.

Sayyid Sadiq al-Mahdi, leader from 1986 to
1989.

Omar Hassan al-Bashir, president since 1989.

GLOSSARY

emme ("EM-ah")
An Arab man's turban.

faki ("FAY-ki")
Teacher-magicians who practice tribal medicine among the Fallata Umboro people of western Sudan.

ful ("FOOL")
A dish made from cooked beans.

haboob ("ha-BOOB")
A sudden sandstorm that occurs in central and northern Sudan.

hashab ("HASH-ab")
A dessert made of chopped bananas, figs, and raisins.

jallabiya ("CHAL-a-bee-ah")
A loose cotton shirt worn by Arab men.

jihad ("ji-HAHD")
Islamic holy war.

kisra ("KISS-rah")
Sudanese unleavened bread, made from sorghum.

lingua franca ("LING-gwa FRAN-ka")
A common language used by groups of people who speak different languages.

mahdi ("MAH-dee")
A Muslim religious leader or savior.

muezzin ("MU-ez-in")
Mosque official whose call to prayer broadcast to worshipers is made at prescribed times.

oud ("OOD")
Musical instrument with five strings, the forerunner of the lute, played with plectrum or fingers.

Ramadan ("RAHM-ah-dahn")
The ninth month of the Islamic calender, when Muslims must refrain from eating or drinking between dawn and dusk.

seiko ("SAY-koh")
An alcoholic drink made from dates.

shariah law ("sha-RI-ah")
Islamic law, introduced throughout Sudan by President Nimeiry in 1983.

shorba ("SHOR-bah")
Lamb soup, a common dish in northern Sudan.

souk ("SOOK")
The city or village market.

SPLA
Southern People's Liberation Army, the army fighting for political rights in the south.

tobe ("TOH-bay")
A long piece of thin fabric worn over clothes to cover the head and body, worn by many women in northern Sudan.

BIBLIOGRAPHY

Asher, Michael. *A Desert Dies*. New York, St. Martin's Press, 1987.

Lonely Planet Guide to Egypt and Sudan. Melbourne: Lonely Planet Publications, 1988.

Voll, John Obert and Sarah Potter Voll. *The Sudan: Unity and Diversity in a Multicultural State.* Boulder: Westview Press, 1985.

Worrall, Nick. *Sudan*. Charles River, 1981; Morrimack, 1984.

INDEX

INDEX

INDEX

PICTURE CREDITS

Andes Press Agency: 48, 51, 72, 107
Camera Press: 38, 53, 55, 121
Susanna Burton: 47, 50, 103 (bottom)
Hulton Deutsch: 26, 27 (top)
Hutchison Library: 4, 10, 11, 12, 13, 20, 25, 29, 32, 33, 37, 39, 56, 58, 59, 61, 63, 66, 68, 71, 75, 76, 78, 79, 82, 83, 84, 86, 89, 90, 92, 95, 100, 101, 103 (top), 104, 105, 106, 111, 116, 120, 123
Image Bank: 16
Björn Klingwall: 23, 30, 52, 64, 67, 85, 93, 108
Christine Osborne: 1, 7, 8, 14, 15, 17, 27 (bottom), 28, 40, 42, 44, 46 (right), 49, 65, 74, 91, 97, 99, 102, 110, 113, 117
Reuters Visnews Library: 69
Peter Sanders: 3, 5, 18, 19, 22, 24, 31, 34, 35, 41, 43, 57, 62, 70, 80, 94, 96, 112, 114, 115, 119
Liba Taylor: 6, 45, 46 (left), 54, 60, 73